U.S. Policy Toward China

BOOKS + ZINES
1415 Knowlton St. Cincinnati
www.soapboxbooks.org

U.S. Policy Toward China

An Introduction to the Role of Interest Groups

Robert G. Sutter

ROWMAN & LITTLEFIELD PUBLISHERS, INC.
Lanham • Boulder • New York • Oxford

ROWMAN & LITTLEFIELD PUBLISHERS, INC.

Published in the United States of America
by Rowman & Littlefield Publishers, Inc.
4720 Boston Way, Lanham, Maryland 20706

12 Hid's Copse Road
Cumnor Hill, Oxford OX2 9JJ, England

British Library Cataloguing in Publication Information Available

Library of Congress Cataloging-in-Publication Data

Sutter, Robert G.
    U.S. policy toward China : an introduction to the role of interest groups / Robert G. Sutter.
       p.   cm.
    Includes bibliographical references and index.
    ISBN 0-8476-8724-4 (cloth : alk. paper). —ISBN 0-8476-8725-2 (paper : alk. paper)
    1. United States—Foreign relations—China. 2. China—Foreign relations—United States. 3.
United States—Foreign relations—1989- 4. Pressure groups—United States—History—20th
century. I. Title.
    E183.8.C5S885 1998
    327.73051—dc21

                                 98-25278
                                     CIP
ISBN 0-8476-8724-4 (cloth : alk. paper)
ISBN 0-8476-8725-2 (pbk. : alk. paper)

Printed in the United States of America

♾™ The paper used in this publication meets the minimum requirements of American
National Standard for Information Sciences—Permanence of Paper for Printed Library
Materials, ANSI Z39.48–1984.

Contents

Chapter 1

Introduction

With the collapse of the U.S. consensus over China policy following the 1989 Tiananmen incident and the end of the cold war, the president and his close advisers have had great difficulty in formulating a policy toward the People's Republic of China (PRC) that would be readily accepted in the United States. President Bush tried to keep China policy under his control and to move U.S. relations with China in directions that he deemed constructive. Yet he and his administration were repeatedly criticized by Congress, the media, and organized groups with differing interests in policy toward the PRC. Some political observers believe that Bush's China policy became a distinct liability—even a deciding factor—to the president in his bid for re-election in 1992.[1]

President-elect Clinton had a clear stance designed to link Chinese behavior on human rights issues with U.S. trade benefits to China, especially most-favored-nation (MFN) tariff treatment. Majorities in Congress and many organized nongovernmental groups favored this position. However, the policy came under increasing pressure from other groups and their allies in Congress and in the administration strongly concerned with U.S. business interests vis-à-vis China. The policy of linkage was abandoned in mid-1994.[2]

The president's decision did not end the battle among competing U.S. groups. Pro-Taiwan interests mobilized in early 1995 to change the administration's position and allow the Taiwan president to travel to the United States in a private capacity. After assuring China that no visa would be granted, President Clinton decided to allow the visit. His reversal immediately triggered a major crisis and military face-off between the United States and China over Taiwan in 1995-1996.[3]

Subsequently, Clinton's administration showed more resolve in pursuing a policy of "engagement" with Chinese leaders. Reassured by generally positive U.S. attention, Chinese leaders responded in kind, leading to the Sino-American official summit in Washington, D.C., in late October 1997. However, debate over U.S. policy toward China continued. Critics and representatives of U.S. groups opposed to Chinese policies or U.S. accommodation of China dogged the summit events and promoted legislative and other actions supporting their positions.

A wide range of organized groups have been active in the making of recent U.S. China policy. These groups are able to play a greater role in influencing U.S. policy because of the greater fluidity and pluralism in U.S. foreign policy, including policy toward China, in the post-cold war period.

The central debates in U.S. China policy during the 1990s have focused on using economic and other leverage to sanction the PRC for human rights abuses or other infractions of U.S.-backed norms. Interest groups comprising businesses, organized labor, human rights organizations, religious groups, Chinese students, Tibetan activists, scholars, and retired U.S. officials have weighed in, as have the governments of China, Taiwan, Hong Kong, Britain, and Japan. Lobbying groups have pressed their case with the administration and Congress. Some have been less interested in changing China policy than in using China-related issues for U.S. partisan political reasons.

In the case of U.S. policy on Taiwan, activists have included representatives of the Taiwan government and other political-economic leaders in Taiwan, Taiwanese-American groups and their allies, and those in the United States favoring Taiwan's independence, including some in Congress. Mustered against them are business and other groups concerned with Beijing's reaction, but the opposition has been led by the State Department and related executive-branch experts charged with managing U.S.-China relations.

Groups that took an interested but secondary role included a wide range of educational, religious, public affairs, and other organizations that have conducted studies, issued reports, and held events designed to deepen U.S. understanding of China. Most have avoided taking positions on sensitive issues, though their publications, seminars, and other events have featured various and often-conflicting views on appropriate policy toward China.[4]

Scholars, media commentators, and other observers have ascribed various degrees of influence to different lobby or interest groups at different times during this period.[5] Thus, Chinese students in the United States were reportedly important in arguing for a tougher U.S. policy in the months after the Tiananmen incident. U.S. farm and grain-exporting groups were essential to President Bush's efforts in 1991 to sustain his veto of legislation placing strict conditions on continued MFN treatment for China.[6] President Clinton's decision to de-link MFN and China's human rights practices in 1994 reflected strong efforts by representatives of the U.S. business community with interests in China. Furthermore, the president's decision to reverse his administration's policy and allow Taiwan's president to visit the United States came in response to efforts by a coalition of pro-Taiwan forces led by the Taiwan government office in Washington, D.C., and lobbyists hired by Taiwan leaders.[7]

Few scholars argue that such lobby or organized groups were the sole or dominant force behind these decisions. Indeed, their influence at particular times has depended on fluctuating circumstances, including changes in elite and public opinion, international pressures and opportunities, and other factors.[8] Measuring the influence of individual interest or lobby groups on U.S. China policy remains a subjective exercise. Nonetheless, a review of the highlights in U.S. decisionmaking on China policy in recent years clearly points to the growing influence of such groups.

This overview of the role of organized groups on the conduct of recent U.S. China policy first introduces in Chapter 2 the greater pluralism and fluidity in U.S. foreign policy in general, and policy toward China in particular, after the cold war. With this development as a backdrop, the chapter then explores the rising complexity and influence of organized groups in the making of U.S. policy and discusses how these conditions favor greater participation of such groups in the policy process. It also provides an overview based on existing scholarship of the types of organized groups that typically influence U.S. foreign policy, the circumstances under which such interest groups are likely to be influential, and implications for U.S. government leaders with responsibility for making and conducting foreign policy. It concludes that even though recent trends give organized U.S. interests or lobbying groups more influence, U.S. policymakers must avoid catering to such groups. Good policy will continue to require careful attention to important international as well as domestic concerns.

Chapters 3 and 4 review the annual executive-congressional debates during the Bush and the first Clinton administrations on whether to grant MFN tariff treatment to Chinese imports freely, conditionally, or not at all. They assess the role of organized groups in influencing what are acknowledged as the most important China policy decisions during this period. Chapter 5 discusses the role of organized groups in determining U.S. policy toward Taiwan seen in the Clinton administration's approval of the Taiwan president's visit to Cornell University in June 1995 and the resulting crisis in U.S.-PRC-Taiwan relations. Chapter 6 assesses the convergence among U.S. administration leaders over China policy and the continuing strong debate over China policy in the Congress, the media, and elsewhere in U.S. society between 1996 and the U.S.-China summit of October 1997. An appendix provides brief profiles of some organized groups with an interest in China policy. Peter Mitchener provided initial drafts for most of the items in the appendix. There is also a chronology and list of selected readings on recent U.S.-China relations and the role of interest groups in U.S. foreign policy.

My analysis focuses on the following arguments:

- U.S. domestic interest groups are now much more important in making U.S. policy toward China than they were during the cold war.

- President Bush strongly resisted U.S. groups endeavoring to push China policy in directions he opposed. He preserved his China policy but lost the election of 1992, in part because of the way he dealt with the PRC.

- President Clinton in his first term was much less concerned with China policy than President Bush and much more accommodating to U.S. interest groups seeking to influence China policy. Vacillation and uncertainty put the administration in a passive position, responding to a tug-of-war between competing U.S. groups over important issues such as MFN for China and U.S. relations with Taiwan. This vacillation led to a serious crisis with the PRC over Taiwan in early 1996 that pushed the White House to take greater control over the conduct of China policy.

- President Clinton entered his second term with a firmer commitment to a more coherent China policy. His policy weakened in the first half of 1997 in the face of strong U.S. domestic criticism and political charges that the administration's policy was influenced by campaign contributions from U.S. and foreign donors eager to promote better U.S. relations with China. As a result, the administration's policy was again heavily influenced by the continuing tug-of-war among competing U.S. groups. Debate continued through the U.S.-China summit of October 1997, at which time the president strongly reaffirmed his policy of "engagement" with the PRC.

- Although the charges of illicit Chinese government and other contributions to U.S. political campaigns stoked the fires of the China policy debate in 1997, available evidence indicates that they played at best a secondary role in the key decisions on China policy. Conventional (and perhaps unconventional) Chinese government efforts to influence U.S. government policy increased markedly in the mid-1990s. They had an overall positive effect in 1995 and 1996 before becoming an issue of controversy in 1997. Nonetheless, much more important in determining U.S. policy was the battle among competing U.S. interests using lobbying tactics and other legal means to persuade policymakers to support their points of view.

- The lessons of the recent experience remind U.S. leaders that they need to consider both domestic and foreign imperatives in making foreign policy. As Robert Putnam points out, foreign policymaking is a "two-level game." U.S. leaders need to be sensitive to the more important role of domestic interests in the post-cold war environment. Otherwise, they may fall from power as did George Bush. At the same time, they need to understand how their actions are perceived internationally. Otherwise, they may find that following U.S. domestic pressures will lead them into a confrontation with a great power like China. (This is what happened to President Clinton when he bowed to domestic U.S. pressures and gave a visa to the Taiwan president in 1995.) Striking a proper balance will be difficult; there is no consensus on U.S. foreign policy direction in the post-cold war era, the U.S. debate over China policy remains very strong, and future actions of a rapidly rising world power that may challenge the international status quo are hard to predict.

Implications for Future U.S.-China Relations

The lessons of recent experience in U.S.-China relations also have implications for those concerned with the outlook for the relationship. Yet specialists in the United States, China, and elsewhere differ over the outlook for U.S.-China relations over the next year.[9]

On the one hand, some optimists judge that the Clinton administration's policy of "engagement" with Chinese leaders resulted in productive Sino-American summit meetings in Washington in October 1997 and will lead to equally fruitful summit meetings in Beijing in 1998. In this view, the two governments are using these and other opportunities to consolidate common ground on economic, environmental, regional security (e.g., Korean peninsula), and other issues, while making progress on various human rights, trade, weapons-proliferation, and other questions that divide them.

Chinese President Jiang Zemin is fresh from his successful re-election at the Chinese Communist Party's 15th Congress in September 1997; he is expected to be more willing and able than in the past to reach compromises on issues important to the United States. Bill Clinton is said to be focused on the long-term importance for the United States, and also for his presidency, of effectively managing China's emergence in world affairs. Thus, the U.S. president is thought by some specialists to be ready to make compromises and gestures aimed at promoting forward movement in relations with China and thereby facilitating China's integration into constructive international relations.

On the other hand are specialists who argue that progress in Sino-American relations will be limited in the short term, and possibly longer, because of constraints and trends in both countries. In this view, Chinese leaders, headed by President Jiang, do not have sufficient will or power needed to reach major breakthroughs with the United States on the various issues—human rights, trade, weapons proliferation, and others—that divide the two governments. These specialists believe the Clinton administration is constrained by a continuing barrage of opposition from influential leaders in the Congress, the media, and elsewhere in U.S. public affairs.

Past patterns of behavior are not always good indicators of future behavior. Nonetheless, a careful review of developments in U.S.-China relations since the Tiananmen incident of 1989 appears to support the arguments of those who are more pessimistic than optimistic about substantial progress in U.S.-China relations over the next year.[10]

Although Chinese officials hold different views of U.S. China policy, at bottom senior Chinese leaders remain deeply suspicious. At times, at least some Chinese leaders suspect that the United States is intent on "containing" China and "holding back" its rise in international power and influence. More uniformly, Chinese leaders view the United States as determined to maintain its status as the world's only superpower and a dominant strategic power in East Asia and to maintain strong ties with Taiwan and support for the island against military pressure from the mainland.

They also are more uniform in suspicion of a long-term U.S. effort—publicly articulated by President Clinton in his opening second-term press conference,[11] and by President Bush before him—to seek to change China's political system along lines compatible with U.S. interests.[12] Meanwhile, Chinese leaders in recent years have followed broad internal and international policies that enjoy support among various segments of the Chinese leadership, often as a result of protracted Chinese leadership negotiations.[13] As a result, Beijing is not inclined to change policy to accommodate the United States.

Beijing has made several adjustments in policy and practice in recent years in ways that favor U.S. interests and facilitate progress in Sino-U.S. relations. However, it has generally done so when the costs of not changing have outweighed the costs of change. Thus, when Chinese leaders feared China might lose U.S. most-favored-nation tariff treatment in 1990 and 1991, they made several last-minute but important concessions on sensitive human rights, proliferation, and other issues in order to buttress U.S. support for continued MFN. Later, when U.S. and world opinion pressed China on the issue of the Comprehensive Nuclear Test Ban, China changed its stance in order to avoid isolation and possible sanction.[14] China also agreed several times to accommodate the United States on market access, intellectual property rights, and other trade issues when it was clear that the alternative was loss of several billion dollars in trade. When China realized that cutting official ties with the United States after Taiwan President Lee Teng-hui's visit to the United States in June 1995 was hurting Chinese interests without much likelihood of concessions from the United States, Beijing returned its ambassador and resumed normal relations. Similar cost-benefit analysis seemed to lie behind Beijing's decision in 1997 to curb nuclear exchanges with Iran and other states for the sake of winning U.S. agreement to revive the moribund U.S.-China nuclear cooperation agreement of 1985.

In the 1990s, Beijing's confidence in its own economic power and its growing standing in world affairs has grown. At the same time, Chinese leaders have become increasingly aware of—and able to use to their own advantage—the sharp divisions in the United States over policy toward China. For example, some U.S. business organizations and some groups representing interests important to the United States in Hong Kong and other parts of Asia have been aggressive in countering the arguments of U.S. critics of China's policies and practices. The result has allowed Beijing to offset pressures from the United States pushing for changes in the Chinese government's policies and practices over human rights, proliferation, trade, and other sensitive issues.

On the U.S. side of the equation, China's inertia and resistance to change in policy areas of concern to the United States add to the arsenal of those who, critical of Chinese policies and practices, are likely to continue to press hard for strong U.S. efforts to promote changes in China. These officials also appear likely to continue to receive strong support from U.S. media, interest groups, and others who strongly disapprove of China's behavior. Ironically, Chinese government inertia also means that U.S. critics will likely face few immediate negative consequences from China for their attacks.

On the former point, it is logical that U.S. officials and others concerned with various disputes with China will see China's continued reluctance to change as an argument for tougher U.S. policy. On the latter point, it is also logical that because China follows current policies for its own reasons—deeply rooted in protracted Chinese leadership deliberations over how they protect and enhance China's interests—Beijing is not likely to change them significantly for the sake of "punishing" China critics in the United States. Indeed, China continues to be solicitous of numerous congressional members who are sharply critical of China, urging them to visit China for meetings with high-level Chinese leaders.

Meanwhile, the Clinton administration thus far has given little sign that it is prepared to take concrete action against congressional and other critics of its policy of engagement toward China. Some specialists criticize the administration for not doing enough either to rally U.S. supporters of its engagement policy or to sanction those Americans who attack and criticize the policy.

In sum, trends in Chinese and U.S. decisionmaking since the Tiananmen incident add to evidence that leaders in both countries had difficulty making substantial progress in their high-level meetings in 1997 and 1998. Chinese leaders are deeply suspicious of many of the changes advocated by the United States, more confident of their power and influence in world affairs and of their ability to turn sharp divisions in the United States to their advantage, and determined to follow policies reached after often protracted efforts to achieve consensus among diverse Chinese leaders. Trends indicate that the many official and unofficial U.S. critics of China's policies and practices have ample incentives and few immediate disincentives for continuing their harsh attacks against Chinese government behavior and the Clinton administration's engagement policy.

The U.S. and Chinese governments *could* choose to depart from recent patterns to achieve a significant breakthrough in Sino-American relations in the next year. Thus, as noted earlier, some specialists are optimistic that the senior leaders will see their interests well served by summit meetings marked by major improvements in the relationship. The leaders may be able to use a sense of common U.S.-Chinese concern over the Asian financial crisis and, perhaps, the controversy over UN weapons inspection in Iraq to offset the critics and their arguments. On balance, however, the pattern of decision-making on both sides in recent years reflects important constraints to seeking greater flexibility, compromise, and advancement in U.S.-China relations.

Notes

1. See, among others, *United States and China Relations at a Crossroads*, Atlantic Council of the United States/National Committee on U.S.-China Relations (Lanham, Md.: University Press of America, 1995).

2. For background see Kerry Dumbaugh, *China-U.S. Relations*, U.S. Congressional Research Service (CRS) Issue Brief 94002 (updated monthly).

3. For background see Robert Sutter, *Taiwan: U.S. Policy Choices,* CRS Issue Brief 96032 (updated monthly).

4. See the appendix for a listing of several such educational and public affairs organizations.

5. See sources in notes below. See also selected readings, below, for a list of sources dealing with interest groups and U.S. foreign policy.

6. See, among others, Jim Mann, "America and China's MFN Benefits: 1989-1994," draft paper distributed at American Assembly Working Group Meeting, February 1995.

7. See, among others, I Yuan, "Tyranny of the Status Quo: The Taiwan Lobby's Impact on U.S.-Taiwan Relations," conference paper, George Washington University, June 17, 1995.

8. See, among others, Randall Ripley and James Lindsay, eds., *Congress Resurgent: Foreign and Defense Policy on Capitol Hill* (Ann Arbor, Mich.: University of Michigan Press, 1993).

9. These judgments are based on consultations with over 100 specialists in China, Japan, South Korea, England, and the United States during 1997. For background on some of those consultations, see CRS Memoranda for Congressional China Watchers dated June 10 and July 8, 1997. For background on recent U.S.-China relations, see Kerry Dumbaugh, *China-U.S. Relations,* CRS Issue Brief 94002.

10. Those interested in more detail on this period can consult the discussion below as well as *China: Interest Groups and Recent U.S. Policy—An Introduction,* by Robert Sutter, CRS Report 97-48 F, 1-62, and David M. Lampton, "America's China Policy in the Age of the Finance Minister," *The China Quarterly* (1994): 597-621.

11. See coverage in *New York Times,* January 30, 1997, 20.

12. For recent background on such Chinese suspicions, see CRS Memorandum for Congressional China Watchers of July 8, 1997.

13. For background on Chinese decisionmaking, see, among others, *China after Deng Xiaoping,* CRS Issue Brief 93114.

14. For background on Chinese weapons proliferation policies and practices, see Shirley Kan, *Chinese Proliferation of Weapons of Mass Destruction,* CRS Report 96-767 F.

Chapter 2

Rising Influence after the Cold War

Post-Cold War Debate in U.S. Foreign Policy

The absence of a clear direction in U.S. policy toward China has broader roots than the vagaries of U.S. China policy. Specifically, some argue that perhaps a more experienced president, one with a clearer vision of Asia policy and a greater election mandate than the 43 percent of the popular vote gained by Bill Clinton in 1992, would have been more decisive in formulating China policy. On the one hand, it is argued that such a president could set a course of action and stick to it—thereby avoiding the repeated tugs-of-war among competing interests. On the other hand, since the end of the cold war, Americans have been deeply divided over foreign policy, and contending policy perspectives cannot easily be bridged to develop coherent policy toward China or indeed other important areas.[1] President Bush, who had a clear view of China policy and followed it, found his policy assailed from various sides in the more fluid and pluralistic foreign policy debates that emerged after the cold war.

Because security issues and opposition to Soviet expansion no longer drive U.S. foreign policy, economic interest, democratization abroad, and human rights have gained greater prominence. Various pressure groups and other institutions interested in these and other subjects also have enhanced influence in policymaking. Historically, such fluidity and competition among priorities have more often than not been the norm. Woodrow Wilson and Franklin Roosevelt both set forth comprehensive concepts of a well-integrated U.S. foreign policy, but neither framework lasted long. The requirements of the cold war were much more effective in establishing rigor and order in U.S. foreign policy priorities, but that era is over.

In particular, the post-cold war period has seen substantial changes in the way foreign policy is made in the United States. In general, there has been a shift away from the elitism of the past and toward much greater pluralism. This increases the opportunity for input by nongovernmental or lobby groups with interests in foreign policy.

The elitist model of foreign policymaking includes the following characteristics:

- Domination of the process by the executive branch, particularly by the White House, the State Department, and the Pentagon.
- Presidential consultation with a bipartisan leadership in Congress and mobilization through them of broad congressional support for the administration's foreign policy.
- Parallel consultations with a relatively small group of elites outside government, some of whom are specialists on the particular issue under consideration and others of whom have a more general interest in foreign policy as a whole.
- Mobilization of public support through the major newspapers and television programs, other media outlets, and civic organizations.[2]

Gradually, however, this process has been transformed in much more pluralistic directions to take on quite different characteristics:

- A much greater range of agencies within the executive branch involved in foreign policy, with the rise of the economic agencies (Commerce, Treasury, and U.S. Trade Representative [USTR]) of particular importance.
- A seeming reallocation of power within government, away from the executive branch and toward Congress.
- Much greater participation by nongovernmental organizations and lobbying groups, which attempt to shape foreign policy to conform with their interests.
- Much less consensus within Congress, and within the broader public, over foreign policy.

There *is* consensus that foreign policy should not be expensive. The recent fate of the international-affairs budget in the U.S. Congress indicates that Americans want foreign policy both to cost less and to give more benefit. Unfortunately, there is little agreement on how to accomplish this objective. Few Americans are aware that foreign policy spending accounts for less than one percent of the federal budget. There appear to be at least three different tendencies or schools of thought regarding post-cold war foreign policy. These approaches are not necessarily exclusive. In particular, a U.S. leader may demonstrate aspects of one tendency at some times and aspects of another tendency at other times. An understanding of what these schools stand for underscores how difficult it is to gauge the direction of U.S. policy toward China or other key areas of international concern.[3]

One prominent school stresses a relative decline in U.S. power and its implication for U.S. ability to protect its interests. It calls for the United States to work harder to preserve important interests while adjusting to limited resources and reduced influence. Advocates of this position expect continued international instability and limited U.S. ability to respond. They observe that there is no international framework to shape policy; that U.S. policy must use a complex mix of international, regional, and bilateral efforts to achieve policy goals; and that security, economic, and cultural-political issues will compete for priority in policymaking. They argue that in this uncertain environment, pressing domestic problems will take precedence over attention to international affairs and restrict financial resources available for foreign policy, defense, and international security. They also believe that policymaking will remain difficult because the executive branch may well remain in control of one political party and Congress in control of the other party.

This school—reflected in the commentary of such leaders as George Bush, Henry Kissinger, and others—argues that these circumstances require the United States to work closely with traditional allies and associates. Regarding Asia, it contends that it is inconsistent with U.S. goals not to preserve long-standing good relations with Japan and other friends and allies in Asia whose security policies and political-cultural orientations complement U.S. interests. It acknowledges that opinion surveys indicate that the public and some leaders have from time to time seen Japan as an economic "threat" but stresses that few polls reflect support for a confrontational foreign policy. It urges caution in policy toward other regional powers—Russia, China, and India. All three countries are preoccupied with internal political-development issues and do not appear to want regional instability. All seek closer economic and political relations with the West and with other advancing economies. Washington would be well-advised, they say, to work closely with these governments wherever there are common interests. In considering U.S. assets available to influence regional trends, they call on the United States to go slow in reducing its regional military presence. The economic savings of cutbacks would be small; the political costs could be high insofar as most countries in Asia encourage the United States to remain active in the region to offset the growing power of Japan or China.

A second school argues for major cutbacks in U.S. international activity, including military involvement, and a renewed focus on solving such domestic problems as crime, drug use, economic competitiveness, educational standards, homelessness, poverty, decaying cities, and transportation infrastructure. Variations of this view are seen in the writings of William Hyland, Patrick Buchanan, and other well-known commentators and in the political statements of Ross Perot. Often called an "America First" or "Neoisolationist" school, it contends that the United States has become overextended in world affairs and has been taken advantage of in the current world security-economic system. It calls for sweeping cuts in spending for international activities, favoring a U.S. pullback from foreign bases and major cuts in foreign assistance and foreign technical-information programs. It is skeptical of the utility of international financial institutions and the United Nations and of international efforts to promote free trade through the World Trade Organization (WTO). It advocates termination of international economic talks that help to perpetuate a liberal world trading system that in practice increases U.S. economic dependence and injures some American workers and industries. Some favor trade measures that are seen as protectionist by U.S. trading partners.

A third position argues that policy needs to promote U.S. interests in international political, military, and economic affairs more actively and to use U.S. influence to pressure countries that do not conform to the norms of an appropriate world order. Supporters of this position want the United States to maintain military forces with worldwide capabilities, to lead strongly in world affairs, and to minimize compromises and accommodations.

This school of thought has been present in American politics throughout this century. However, for several reasons it is stronger today than at any time since the 1960s. During the Reagan administration, after a prolonged period of introspection and doubt following the Vietnam War, oil shocks, and the Iran hostage crisis, the American public became much more optimistic about the future of the United States. This trend was reinforced by the end of the cold war, a victory for the U.S.-backed system of collective security and for U.S. political and economic values. The outcome of the 1991 Persian Gulf War with Iraq further inspired confidence in U.S. military doctrine, equipment, and performance and in America's international leadership ability.

Those who support this view acknowledge that America faces serious economic challenges, but they are optimistic that the United States can succeed in a competitive world economy. They also insist that the United States is better positioned than any other country to exert leadership in the realm of ideas and values, political concepts, lifestyle, popular culture, and international organizations. They perceive a global power vacuum, caused notably by the collapse of the Soviet empire, which allows the United States to exert influence. They are undeterred by warnings of declining U.S. government economic, military, and other resources. They argue that Russia, China, and India will remain preoccupied with domestic problems. They acknowledge that Japan and Germany are economically powerful but also uncertain how to use their power and that they lack American cultural attractiveness and influence.[4]

In recent years, advocates of this third tendency have been most vocal in pressing for a strong policy in support of democracy and human rights. They have argued for a more active foreign policy, which has led some targeted countries to view U.S. policy as interference in other countries' internal affairs. They have opposed economic or trading policies of other countries seen as inequitable or predatory. They have pressed for a strong policy against proliferation of weapons of mass destruction. Members of this school also argue variously for sanctions against countries that practice coercive birth control, seriously pollute the environment, or harbor terrorists and promote the drug trade. They believe the United States should be more assertive in promoting humanitarian relief and in recognizing the legitimacy of people's right to self-determination.

Three Approaches to U.S.-China Policy

In recent years members of the third group—advocates of active U.S. leadership—have been most forceful in calling for policies opposing Chinese human rights violations, weapons proliferation, and protective trade practices. They have pressed Beijing to meet U.S.-backed international norms and called for retaliatory economic sanctions. By contrast, the more cautious and accommodating first group often believes that the advocates of strong assertion of U.S. values are unrealistic about U.S. power and unwilling to make needed compromises with the Chinese government to protect U.S. interests and regional stability and avoid strategic enmity.[5]

It is unclear which of these approaches will ultimately have the greatest influence on China policy. Some in the Clinton administration and in Congress advocate the moderate, less confrontational posture of "engagement" with China. Concerned with perceived weaknesses in China, some urge a moderate policy for fear that to do otherwise could promote divisions in and a possible breakup of China with potentially adverse consequences for U.S. interests in Asian stability and prosperity. Impressed by China's growing economic and national strength, others seek the opportunities this provides for the United States. They promote U.S. engagement in order to guide China's powers into channels of international activity compatible with American interests.

In general, this moderate approach believes that trends in China are moving inexorably in the "right" direction—that China is increasingly interdependent economically with its neighbors and the advanced industrial economies and thus increasingly unlikely to destabilize these relationships. Economic growth promotes a materially better-off and more educated and cosmopolitan populace that will, over time, press for greater political pluralism and democratic institutions; U.S. policy should work closely with China to encourage these long-term trends.

A second, tougher approach is advocated by some inside and outside of the U.S. government who doubt the interdependence argument laid out above. They stress that PRC officials still view the world as a state-centered, competitive environment where interdependence could compromise Chinese power and entangle its sovereignty. In this view, China's leaders are determined to "use any means" to increase Chinese wealth and power. At present, Beijing is merely biding its time, conforming to many international norms to build its economic and technological strength; once it succeeds with economic modernization, Beijing will not sacrifice nationalistic and territorial ambitions for economic stability. U.S. leaders should be firm with China. Rather than try to persuade Beijing of the advantages of cooperation, the United States should rely on military power as a counterweight to rising Chinese power, remain firm in dealing with economic and security conflicts, and work closely with traditional allies and friends along China's periphery to deal with Chinese assertiveness.

A third approach favored by some U.S. officials and other leaders believes that China's political system needs to change before the United States can establish a constructive relationship with Beijing. China's communist leaders are inherently incapable of participating in cooperative relationships and U.S. policy should aim to change China from within while maintaining vigilance against disruptive Chinese foreign policy. U.S. policy should not abet the development of an authoritarian superpower more advanced economically than the former Soviet Union and controlling a population four times as large.

Interest Groups That Influence U.S.-China Policy

Combined with the lack of consensus and fluidity in U.S. foreign policy after the cold war, the ongoing debate among advocates of the three competing approaches to China provides fertile ground for organized groups. In particular, competing policy proponents strive hard to muster recruits into coalitions backing their particular concerns. In recent years, these have included issues like human rights, trade disputes, weapons-proliferation questions, and others. Competing coalitions have fought bitterly, especially during major crises such as the decisions of the Bush and Clinton administrations to grant MFN tariff treatment to mainland China and of the Clinton administration to upgrade U.S. interaction with Taiwan—particularly the president's May 1995 decision allowing Taiwan President Lee Teng-hui to travel in a private capacity to Cornell University.

In general, organized American interest groups concerned with foreign policy can be divided among those dealing with economic interests, specific values or causes, ethnic issues, and issues important to foreign governments and foreign economic interests. Within the economic realm, major business groups include the National Association of Manufacturers, the Chamber of Commerce, and the Business Roundtable. They endeavor to promote such general business concerns as foreign trade. Also very influential are groups such as the Emergency Committee for American Trade, which has worked to ensure that the United States would continue to grant MFN tariff treatment to China.[6]

Trade associations related to a specific industry or to businesses working in a particular part of the world have influenced U.S. foreign policy, as have industries themselves. The U.S.-China Business Council and the Boeing Corporation are good examples.

Sometimes countering the positions of business interest groups are those representing organized labor. Labor unions in recent years are linked with a more trade-restrictive stance; they sometimes view Chinese exports to the United States as a threat to U.S. jobs, and they also have weighed in on a variety of social-justice issues, including human rights and labor rights and the use of prison labor to produce Chinese exports. They hold that U.S. goods cannot be expected to compete against those made using U.S. technology by poorly paid workers in large, subsidized industries without labor, safety, and environmental standards. The AFL-CIO has been strongly critical of Beijing's human-rights practices.[7]

A number of public interest or citizen groups have common concerns of a noneconomic or nonoccupational sort. Many of these organizations focus on a single issue or a small group of issues. Examples include groups concerned with independence or greater autonomy for Tibet (e.g., the International Campaign for Tibet) and the freedom of political prisoners in China (e.g., Asia Watch); religious freedom and freedom from coercive birth control and abortions (e.g., Family Research Council); as well as those concerned with limiting Chinese practices that endanger the regional and international environment or that promote instability and possible conflict through the proliferation of weapons of mass destruction and related technology (e.g., the Wisconsin Project).

Ethnic groups are a key factor in private organizations actively trying to influence U.S. foreign policy. Ethnic "lobbies" have been prominently featured in existing scholarship on U.S. foreign policy. Although Chinese-Americans represent nearly one percent of the U.S. population, they have not become a unified ethnic lobby in U.S. foreign policy politics. However, there have been instances in which segments of this group have been active in U.S. foreign policy politics. Expatriate Chinese students heavily lobbied Congress and the administration during the years immediately following the 1989 Tiananmen incident in Beijing. Their influence quickly waned as the groups became divided over their goals regarding U.S. policy toward China. A much more cohesive ethnic group is made up of the estimated 500,000 Americans who trace their family background to Taiwan. Taiwanese-Americans have formed a variety of organizations that have actively encouraged U.S. foreign policy to respect Taiwan's separate status and autonomy from the mainland. Many in these groups are strong advocates of independence for the island.[8]

Foreign governments and foreign businesses also work actively to influence U.S. foreign policy. Embassies lobby on behalf of their countries' interests; foreign governments and businesses hire professional lobbyists to help them influence U.S. policy. Government, business, and other leaders of Taiwan have been active for many years in pressing their point of view on the U.S. government, especially Congress. A number of press and other reports have linked Taiwanese government and other groups with large U.S. campaign contributions.[9] These proponents have also been prominent in recent years in promoting academic, think-tank, media, local government, and other research and exchanges that enhance goodwill and positive feelings between Taiwan and the United States.

The mainland Chinese government and business leaders have historically been much less active on these fronts, though repeated reports in 1996 and 1997 claimed that the Chinese government was involved in funneling campaign contributions to U.S. candidates in the 1996 election. Chinese government and business leaders also exercise the attraction of vast markets on U.S. manufacturers, investors, traders, and policymakers. They have recently increased efforts to promote exchanges with the Congress, and the Chinese government has worked closely with U.S. businesses that have lobbied effectively for continued MFN trade treatment for China.

When Are Interest Groups Influential in Making U.S. Foreign Policy?

Lobbyists and other advocates representing organized groups and their interests are often quick to note their "impact" on the U.S. policy process. Scholars and analysts are usually inclined to be more cautious in measuring such influence. They recognize that the outcomes of political processes are decided by many factors. Organized interests often are important parts of coalitions that emerge in Washington, especially in Congress, on particular issues, but they are only a part of a larger mix of actors and influences that affect policy decisions.

There are times when organized groups appear more influential on policymaking than at others. Looking at Congress, an arena in which citizens and organizing groups are more easily able to gain access to policymakers than in the executive branch, one can isolate factors that affect the degree of influence exerted by organized interest groups.

Assessing available scholarship on this subject, John Tierney notes the parallels between Congress's influence on foreign policy and that of organized interest groups. He argues that Congress's role (vis-à-vis that of the president) in foreign policy increases as one moves along a spectrum from what he calls crisis policies to strategic policies to structural policies. He traces the same patterns for organized interests. Generally speaking, this means that organized interests have less to say in decisionmaking processes surrounding crises. Yet, in his view, as presidential dominance and "national interest" considerations decline in intensity with movement away from crises along the policy spectrum, the potential for interest-group influence increases.[10]

U.S. behavior toward China in the post-cold war environment seems to bear out this pattern. From this perspective, the U.S.-Soviet conflict of the cold war was in many respects a protracted series of crises. After 1970 the U.S.-China relationship was a key element in U.S. strategy toward the Soviet bloc. China policy afforded few opportunities for pressure from Congress or organized interests contrary to executive leadership. After the cold war, organized interests became much more prominent, as did the role of Congress. Human rights groups, pro-Taiwan movements, economic interest groups, and others have at various times had important influence in the course of U.S. policy.[11]

The nature of the issue makes a difference in determining the influence of organized interests. Organized interests are less likely to be influential, both on highly visible issues that engage widespread, contrary public passions or media coverage and on issues in which there are strong, competing ideological, partisan, or constituency pressures. On the contrary, organized interests appear more likely to affect outcomes on issues that neither undergo active public or media scrutiny nor conflict with legislators' or other policymakers' convictions, partisan leanings, or constituency needs. Meanwhile, just as Congress is more effective in foreign affairs in changing or blocking executive action than in taking major legislative initiatives on its own, so too are organized interests more effective in working to resist or alter changes rather than in actively changing the status quo.

An American Assembly study group on the growing influences of organized interests on U.S. foreign policy cited five sets of techniques used by organized interests that have been effective in influencing U.S. foreign policy after the cold war.[12]

1. *Be active, not reactive:* The American political context today is focused on domestic affairs. To be heard and to be effective, interest groups concerned with foreign policy must take the initiative and seek out opportunities to influence the direction of policy. Otherwise, policymakers will be inclined in general to go along with the political trend and focus on domestic affairs to the exclusion of foreign policy issues.

2. *The message:* Interest groups need to have a clear and cogent message. This message needs to be timed to the needs and considerations of policymakers. The message is easier to deliver if it coincides with an event that forces U.S. policymakers to make a decision. (For example, the annual U.S. government consideration of mainland China's most-favored-nation tariff treatment provides such a decision point for both the president and Congress.[13])

The message needs to clearly identify issues, options, and contingencies. (For example, those pressing for upgrading U.S. relations with Taiwan might address the negative reactions likely to come from Beijing. It probably is not sufficient to assert, as many have done, that Beijing would do little or that managing the U.S.-PRC relationship is not a concern of those urging upgrading of U.S.-Taiwan relations.)

3. *Amplifying the message:* A problem for interest groups is how to gain media attention for their message. Favorable media coverage can build broader support and increase the amount of funds and other resources available to the interest groups. However, broad media coverage often is not the most effective way to reach a goal. Some interest groups dealing with particularly sensitive issues would rather avoid the media spotlight, which could reflect badly in the public eye on their efforts to seek particular actions in American foreign policy.

Other ways of amplifying the message include using local governmental and other grass roots efforts to boost support for a particular cause. (For example, state governments, large cities, and other local governments have been especially active recently in seeking economic advantage from international commerce and economic exchange with various areas and countries, including mainland China and Taiwan.)

4. *Entry points:* It is widely held that Congress is a major focus in the government for U.S. interest groups. Members of Congress and their staffs are responsive to constituents and others whose interests have a bearing on their constituents and on their overall record of success or failure in Congress.

The nonhierarchical and nonbureaucratic organization of Congress allows for many different entry points in efforts to influence particular policies. For example, it has not been uncommon for senators and House members not serving on foreign policy committees to have notable influence on policy toward mainland China and Taiwan. Sen. Barry Goldwater is a past example. In recent years, Senators Bradley, McCain, and Nunn provided such leadership. Moreover, since Congress is open and members repeatedly put their views on the record, special interest representatives are able to get a good idea of which members have taken a position and which members are undecided.

Organized interest groups generally have a harder time trying to influence the executive branch. Once foreign policy decisions are made at the cabinet level, the nature of the bureaucracy makes executive branch officials less sensitive to pressures or initiatives from groups outside government. Nevertheless, there are many entry points, especially with political appointees at the senior levels of government. These individuals are more politically attuned because they recognize the need to appear responsive to important interests in the country on particular issues.

State governments and localities can also be helpful in influencing policies—for example, through contacts with their congressional delegations. State and local governments appear to be attentive to the economic impacts of particular moves in foreign affairs.

5. *Strategies:* Key decisions of special interest representatives focus on the proper balance between working with those policymakers likely to be supportive of the organized interest and working with those thought to be skeptical and needing more persuasion. In addition, these groups need to decide whether to stick to a firm, "principled" position on particular issues or to show greater flexibility in the interest of compromise.

Taking a principled stance ensures that a clear message is sent to those concerned, effectively rallying supporters. The moral content of the issue may be a factor in discussions on tactical compromise. A principled hard line also stakes out a strong position that could force the ultimate compromise to move in the desired direction. Yet taking such a firm position risks being seen as extreme or so rigid that the policymakers are inclined to avoid consultation or deliberations with the interest representatives.

A more flexible and accommodating position by the organized groups might increase the chances that policymakers would consult with them on sensitive policy questions. However, such an approach could alienate many of the so-called "true believers" whose support is critical to the special interest representative. These individuals could see compromise as undermining what they believe is the moral righteousness of the issue or movement.

Dealing Effectively with Interest Group Pressures: The Two-level Game

According to Robert Putnam, domestic groups pursue their interests at the national level of government policymaking by pressuring their government to adopt favorable policies. U.S. and other national politicians seek power by constructing coalitions among these interest groups. At the international level, national governments, including the U.S. government, seek to maximize their own ability to satisfy domestic pressures while minimizing the adverse consequences of foreign developments.[14] Each of these levels of what Putnam calls a "two-level game" in U.S. foreign policy is important to decisionmakers.

The difficulties for national leaders, including U.S. government leaders, in reconciling the demands of the two levels may be profound. An example discussed in more detail later relates to the U.S. decision to permit Taiwan's president to visit the United States in 1995. President Clinton was under formidable pressure from U.S. groups that were eager to see the visit of Lee Teng-hui. The Taiwan government, Taiwan business interests, and Taiwanese-American and other organized groups also pressed for the visit.[15] Their efforts and other significant considerations saw nearly unanimous votes in Congress in favor of resolutions supporting the Lee Teng-hui visit.

The president realized that a decision to grant Lee a visa would be welcomed by the groups pressing him on U.S. domestic politics, and internationally it would be welcomed by Taiwan and its supporters in world affairs. Beijing had made known its serious concern about such a visit, however. In the end, President Clinton changed his policy in accord with congressional and other domestic pressure. As a result, he faced the decidedly negative consequences of China's strong and hostile reaction to the visit, culminating in the first face-off between U.S. and PRC military forces in over thirty years.[16]

The ensuing tensions between the United States and China over Taiwan in 1995-1996 graphically illustrated what Putnam and others see as the advantages for U.S. leaders when they can build a package of policy proposals that will be acceptable at both the domestic and international levels of the two-level game. A policy that is out of balance, favoring one level at the expense of the other, runs the risk of serious disruption and other negative consequences.

Suggestions for More Effective Government Decision-making[17]

The retreat of the top-down approach to foreign policy decision-making in the post-cold war period suggests that U.S. government decisionmakers will be taking greater account of the increased role of organized interests and other features of the more pluralistic influences on U.S. foreign policy, including policy toward China. The American Assembly Study Group and others believe that the experience of the crisis caused by the 1995 Lee Teng-hui visit also illustrates that U.S. policymakers may take more careful account of both the "national" and "international" arenas in which their actions have an impact.

The American Assembly study group and other scholars have offered some specific suggestions for U.S. policymakers dealing in the more pluralistic post-cold war foreign policymaking process.[18] The executive branch and those involved in Congress should engage in much earlier and more extensive consultation with relevant interest groups in the formulation of policy. The sustainability of foreign policy, and thus the credibility of the U.S. government abroad, increasingly depends on the government's ability to mobilize and maintain long-term public support. The breadth and depth of that support require a greater degree of public engagement in the process of making policy.

The administration and those involved in Congress should go beyond the traditional approach of mobilizing understanding and support for foreign policy only after that policy has been decided. The earlier that engagement with the public can begin, the better. In recent years, there has been more consultation between the government and relevant organized groups, but this has occurred relatively late in the process—notably, after interdepartmental working groups have already drafted a policy document for consideration by the National Security Council or the National Economic Council. At this point, it is usually too late to make any major changes; there is little opportunity for external advice on the broadest contours of policy.

Second, the administration and those involved in Congress also should reach out beyond the small number of elites with whom they have consulted in the past, or even the interest groups that actively present their policy recommendations for consideration. The executive branch should consult with organizations throughout the nation, rather than focusing only on those with headquarters or representatives in Washington, in order to identify all those with a potential interest in an issue, even if they have not yet begun to express an opinion. For example, the American Assembly concluded that the Clinton administration failed to engage the Vietnamese-American community in decisions involving the normalization of U.S. relations with Hanoi largely because the relevant organizations were not based in Washington and because they had not taken the initiative to present their views to the government. As a result, the executive branch had to "play catch-up" to secure the support of these constituencies with a deep interest in this aspect of foreign policy.

Finally, policymakers in the administration and Congress should not only assess the public mood at the time they formulate policy but also anticipate whether that mood will change over time. Groups originally consulted may change their positions as the situation evolves; other groups may begin to find their interests affected and enter the policymaking process. The failure to make this longer-term assessment helped to explain why the Clinton administration's policy of imposing conditions on China's MFN status lost public support between 1993 and 1994. The administration did not anticipate that the American business community would take such a forceful position in the debate, or that an increasing number of Chinese students in the United States and members of Congress would conclude that sustained engagement with Beijing would be a more effective way of promoting human rights than the imposition of economic sanctions.

Weaknesses of the "Pluralistic" Model. Consultation does not guarantee good policy.[19] The American people and much of the rest of the world presumably prefer a more consistent and clear-cut foreign policy approach by the U.S. government. The United States is obviously the most powerful country in the post-cold war environment; erratic U.S. behavior has potentially dangerous consequences for many at home and abroad. As a result, U.S. policymakers seek a more stable and coherent policy approach. In particular, they are making greater efforts to reach out to and consult with Congress, relevant interest groups and others in developing policy objectives and approaches. Although the process is time consuming for often-busy policymakers, it results in a policy that is more broadly based and sustainable than would otherwise be the case.

However, such broader consultations do not always lead to good policy. Indeed, the Clinton administration worked with Congress and relevant interest groups regarding China policy much more extensively than previous administrations did with many of their "top-down" policies. Yet the result has been policy that seems no better supported in Congress and appears to many as vacillating and erratic.

Some observers argue that U.S. policy toward mainland China and Taiwan appears to be at a point that it needs to draw from the strengths of both the elitist and the pluralistic models. From the elitist approach one would begin with active presidential leadership, rooted in a farsighted definition of the long-term national interest and advised by disinterested experts on complex issues; from the pluralistic model, consultation with Congress and interest groups, with more effective mechanisms for combining divergent interests. Priorities based on U.S. national interests would be defined, publicly articulated, and followed. To make this process work would require civility, forbearance, and some willingness on the part of participants to compromise.

Notes

1. See discussion in, among others, Robert Sutter, *Shaping China's Future in World Affairs* (Boulder, Colo.: Westview Press, 1996), 76-83.

2. This is taken from Harry Harding, *Public Engagement in American Foreign Policy,* The American Assembly, Columbia University, February 23-25, 1995, 8-9.

3. For an analysis, see among others, Charlotte Preece and Robert Sutter, *Foreign Policy Debate in America,* CRS Report 91-833F, November 27, 1991. On the first school, see Henry Kissinger's biweekly article in the *Washington Post.* On the second school, see the opinion articles by Patrick Buchanan published regularly in the *Washington Times.*

4. American proponents of this view often are focused on specific issues such as human rights, trade policy, or proliferation of weapons of mass destruction. One articulation of this school is seen in Joseph Nye, *Bound to Lead* (Cambridge, Mass.: Harvard University Press, 1992).

5. These are reviewed notably in Robert Sutter, *China in World Affairs—U.S. Policy Choices,* CRS Report 95-265, January 29, 1995, 15-18. As in the case of the three schools in U.S. foreign policy, these approaches to China policy are not rigid or exclusive.

6. This framework is taken from John T. Tierney, "Interest Group Involvement in Congressional Foreign and Defense Policy," in *Congress Resurgent,* Randall Ripley and James L. Lindsay, eds. (Ann Arbor, Mich.: University of Michigan Press, 1993), 89-111. For other sources on this issue, see selected readings following.

7. AFL-CIO President Lane Kirkland called for ending U.S. MFN treatment on account of Beijing's human rights violations. See Jim Mann, "America and China's MFN Benefits: 1989-1994," draft paper distributed at American Assembly Working Group Meeting, February 1995.

8. See various Taiwan-American groups, especially the Formosan Association for Public Affairs, listed in the Appendix.

9. See, notably, *Wall Street Journal* and *New York Times,* November 1, 1996.

10. John Tierney, "Interest Group Involvement."

11. Interestingly, for a time in mid-1995, U.S. China policy pivoted on two individuals representing Taiwan and human rights interests respectively. That is, U.S. policy to a remarkable extent hinged on the visit of Lee Teng-hui to the United States and the PRC detention of human rights activist Harry Wu.

12. Harry Harding, *Public Engagement in American Foreign Policy,* The American Assembly, Columbia University, February 23-25, 1995.

13. As an example of seemingly poor timing by advocates, several observers at the American Assembly Study Group pointed out that it might not have been a good idea to press congressional members on support for Taiwan's bid for UN membership in early 1995—a time when Congress was heavily preoccupied with consideration of the Republican-sponsored "Contract with America" during the first 100 days of the 104th Congress. Nonetheless, Taiwan legislators and pro-Taiwan lobbyists pressed for congressional attention at that time. The effort was ultimately in vain. Deliberations, American Assembly Study Group, February 23-25, 1995.

14. The framework for this analysis is taken from Robert Putnam, "Diplomacy and Domestic Politics: The Logic of Two-Level Games," *International Organizations* 42, no. 3 (summer 1988): 427-60.

15. See, among others, Thomas Robinson, "America in Taiwan's Post-Cold War Foreign Relations," *The China Quarterly* 148 (December 1996): 1340-61.

16. See CRS Issue Brief 96032.

17. These are derived in large measure from the deliberations of the American Assembly Study Group, February 23-25, 1995, December 4, 1995.

18. Harry Harding, *Public Engagement in American Foreign Policy.*

19. Based on consultations with the American Assembly Study Group, 1995-1996.

Chapter 3

The MFN Debate during the Bush Administration

The televised Tiananmen crackdown of June 1989 created a major crisis in U.S. policy toward China. President Bush and his aides on the National Security Council staff took the lead in formulating the U.S. response to the crisis. The president took charge personally in dealing with various issues during the next years. He strove hard to maintain a balanced policy that would allow for continued U.S. involvement with the people and leaders of China. He saw sustaining MFN tariff treatment for China as essential for his policy of "engagement."

In the crisis atmosphere, the president appeared to judge that it was important to narrow sharply the circle of officials who would manage U.S. policy toward China.[1] In part, this was because the president was attempting to strike a difficult balance in U.S. policy. On the one hand, he was attempting to elicit positive gestures from Beijing's beleaguered leaders in the wake of Tiananmen. On the other hand, he was attempting to avoid what he judged were overly punitive and counterproductive measures against China, which were being pressed on the administration by leaders in the Congress, media representatives, and organized nongovernmental groups. In order to avoid sending the "wrong signal" to Beijing or to domestic constituencies, the president and his White House staff decided to keep a tight rein on the policy. Most notably, the president and his close advisers planned and executed two high-level missions to Beijing without the knowledge of most U.S. officials, and they took steps to ensure that State Department and other U.S. officials avoided comment on the most sensitive policy issue of 1990—the extension of most-favored-nation tariff treatment to China.[2]

By the end of 1990, the president's policy efforts had succeeded in avoiding any serious congressional challenge to his annual MFN waiver for China, but they had not calmed congressional debate or restored a consensus in U.S.-China policy. Bush was branded in many quarters as minimizing human rights abuses in China, being overly attentive to the interests of Chinese leaders, and stressing excessively China's alleged strategic importance for the United States.

Bush's View of U.S. Policy toward China, 1989

President Bush's determination to maintain firm personal control of U.S. China policy following Tiananmen was rooted in his repeated contention that he "knew" China, was able to deal effectively with Chinese leaders, and had a proper perspective on U.S. policy. In contrast, U.S. critics took issue with these claims. They repeatedly asserted that the president did not have a vision of future U.S. policy toward China that took into account the new realities of the post-cold war environment and the greater importance of human rights in foreign policy. Other charges centered on the president's heavy reliance on advisers like Brent Scowcroft and Lawrence Eagleburger, who led the two secret U.S. missions to Beijing in 1989. Scowcroft and Eagleburger were often associated with the views of former Secretary of State Henry Kissinger, whom critics charged overemphasized China's strategic and economic importance and soft-pedaled U.S. interests in Chinese human rights and political reform. Behind such accusations lay broader charges regarding the president's tendency to be swayed by public opinion polls, his proclivity to be flexible and to make compromises in order to preserve a smooth foreign policy, and his reluctance to fight for the sake of principle.[3]

What must have been particularly frustrating for the president was the fact that the public record has shown that most of these criticisms were far from the mark. Thus, a careful review of publicly available White House documents shows that President Bush at the outset of his administration laid out clearly the broad outlines of his administration's China policy. He used the occasion of his February 1989 official visit to China to offer repeated and often personal reflections on the future course of U.S.-China relations.[4] At that time, the president saw the prospect of a gradually changing China—a communist nation whose growing economic and other interaction with the United States and the developed world would eventually and inevitably lead to greater economic benefit, political benefit, and improved human rights conditions for the people of China. The president considered it crucial for the United States to be involved constructively with this process of change because of China's size, location, economic potential, and strategic importance. He judged that there were likely to be continued Sino-American disputes because of wide differences in respective political, economic, and social systems, but argued that U.S. engagement should continue.

In contrast, U.S. press coverage of the president's visit highlighted two issues and virtually ignored the president's exposition of a comprehensive U.S. policy. The media depicted the visit as a thinly disguised U.S. effort to assess Chinese intentions and solidify U.S.-PRC relations prior to the April 1989 visit of Soviet leader Mikhail Gorbachev to Beijing. They interpreted the president's repeated denials in the face of press queries about the United States' being interested in playing the "China card" during the visit as reflecting angst in the administration over the thaw in Sino-Soviet ties. By far the highlight of U.S. press coverage of the trip, however, came when Chinese security forces prevented Fang Lizhi from attending a U.S. embassy reception for the president, to which the Chinese dissident had been invited. Some media reports emphasized that President Bush was less than firm in complaining about the security forces' actions, alleging that the president's long-standing personal ties with Chinese leaders, going back to his days as head of the U.S. liaison office in Beijing in the mid-1970s, curbed his willingness to complain about such high-handed actions. Reporters pointed out that the Chinese leader Deng Xiaoping had openly favored Bush over his Democratic challenger in the 1988 presidential elections.[5]

To be fair, the president's actions and statements in Beijing could have given the impression to the press that he was not prepared to push strongly on bilateral differences with Chinese leaders. Bush repeatedly characterized the visit as a sort of sentimental journey. It was the fifth time he had returned since leaving as liaison office chief in the mid-1970s; his wife, Barbara, had visited six times in the same period. On several occasions he referred warmly to events that marked his stay in China during the 1970s, noting repeatedly that his daughter had been baptized in China. However, the president also used the occasion of his visit to his former congregation in Beijing to press his case for the gradual improvement of human rights in China, and his keynote speech to the Chinese nation also emphasized this theme. The president's interest in this issue was underlined by the fact that Fang Lizhi was only one of several Chinese dissidents who were invited and actually attended the president's reception at the U.S. Embassy.

The president's statements in China also took due account of the rapidly changing world order and the role of U.S.-Soviet-Chinese relations in the new global environment. China was not seen as a lever against Soviet power. According to the president, it was important because of its size, location, and potential impact on world developments in a host of areas. In effect, the president's remarks attempted to move U.S. policy away from a myopic view of China's strategic importance against the USSR toward one that took account of recent trends of East-West and Sino-Soviet accommodation and served U.S. interests in an emerging world order.

Subsequently, despite all the turmoil in China—and in the United States over U.S.-China policy—following the Tiananmen massacre, Bush remained steadfast in support of his vision of U.S. China policy. Critical American commentators often interpreted the president's actions as reflecting the president's insensitivity to human rights concerns, his overemphasis on China's strategic importance, and his misguided reliance on personal relations with Chinese leaders. In retrospect, a more balanced view would see that the president was consistent in his determination to see that the United States remained involved in China for the sake of human progress there. Although China's strategic and economic importance to the United States was temporarily in decline because of the East-West détente and economic disruption in China, the PRC was of long-term strategic importance to U.S. interests because of its size, potential, and location.

In part because Americans had no opportunity to appreciate Bush's earlier expositions of China policy, his remarks after Tiananmen often were seen as defensive and self-serving. They did not still the widespread grumbling about the president's alleged "bias" toward a "soft" China policy.

The Tiananmen Massacre and U.S. Policy Response

Initial Reaction. The crisis that followed the Tiananmen massacre had several features. Chinese leaders were preoccupied with establishing internal control and stability and dealing with adverse international trends. The latter included the sanctions imposed by the United States, Japan, and the West; the collapse of communism in Europe; and the overthrow of leaders friendly to China, such as Romania's Nicolae Ceausescu. These trends shifted the initiative in Sino-U.S. relations to the United States after mid-1989.

Bush succeeded initially in preserving a general U.S. consensus about China policy when he announced on June 5, 1989, the steps the United States would take in response to the Tiananmen incident. The president ordered the suspension of all government-to-government sales and commercial exports of weapons; suspension of visits between U.S. and Chinese military leaders; and sympathetic review of requests by Chinese students in the United States to extend their stay, among other measures. On June 20, 1989, the administration took the additional steps of directing that the U.S. government suspend participation in all high-level exchanges of governmental officials with China and directing American representatives at various international financial institutions to postpone consideration of new loans for China.

Reflecting strong reaction against China's leaders by U.S. public opinion, media, and human rights organizations and Chinese student groups in the United States, many in Congress pressed for harsher measures. As debate continued into the summer, however, it became clear that congressional legislation on sanctions against China would leave the president considerable room for maneuver. A lengthy amendment on China to the State Department authorization bill, which passed the Senate in late July, codified the sanctions already imposed by the president and added the following suspensions: new programs to guarantee U.S. investments in China, licenses for crime control and detection equipment, export licenses for U.S. satellites scheduled for launch on Chinese launch vehicles, and peaceful nuclear cooperation with China. It also required the president to negotiate with the Coordinating Committee (COCOM) to halt further liberalization of export controls for technology to China. The bill provided waiver authority acceptable to the administration. Meanwhile, in moves during July and August 1989 that reflected the specific interests of the tens of thousands of Chinese students in the United States, the House and Senate respectively passed the Emergency Chinese Immigration Relief Act, which would have made it possible for Chinese students in the United States to extend their stays for up to four years.

The Bush administration and many in Congress privately pressed the Chinese authorities to take actions that would improve the strained atmosphere in Sino-U.S. relations. Suggested steps included easing martial law in Beijing; showing greater flexibility in the case of the dissident Fang Lizhi, who took refuge in the U.S. Embassy; allowing U.S. Fulbright professors to resume work in China; halting periodic jamming of Voice of America (VOA) broadcasts to China; and allowing the U.S. Peace Corps to begin its volunteer program in China. As gestures to China in the interests of preserving U.S.-Chinese relations, the administration in late July 1989 granted waivers to the suspension of military sales to allow the sale of four Boeing commercial jets with navigation systems that could be converted to military use. In October 1989, the administration permitted Chinese military officers to return to work at U.S. facilities where they had been assisting U.S. engineers in upgrading China's F-8 fighter with U.S. avionics. On November 30, the president let it be known that he would pocket veto the Emergency Chinese Immigration Relief Act, maintaining that the bill was unnecessary since he was ordering into practice many of its provisions.

The Uproar over the Scowcroft Missions. Although there was considerable grumbling in Congress and the media over the president's "soft" approach to China, the debate over China policy reached a fever pitch following the December 9-10, 1989, visit to Beijing by a U.S. delegation led by National Security Advisor Scowcroft and the disclosure a few days later that a similar U.S. delegation had secretly visited Beijing in July 1989. Critics in Congress and the media, human rights and Chinese student groups, and others denounced the president's actions and called on Congress to take stronger action when it convened in late January.

Despite the storm of criticism, Bush continued his moderate approach during December. On December 19, he waived restrictions prohibiting export licenses for three U.S. communications satellites to be launched on Chinese space vehicles, and he announced that he would not impose the new restrictions on Export-Import Bank funding for China that Congress had enacted earlier.

As Congress prepared to reconvene in late January 1990 amid a chorus of media comment calling for tougher action against China, it was clear that the president had miscalculated and would have to adjust his policies. For one thing, Chinese leaders had proven unable or unwilling to make gestures to the United States that were seen to be of sufficient importance to justify the president's actions. The Chinese government ended martial law in Beijing but a major police presence remained; some prisoners were released, but only a small fraction of those thought to be held. The Chinese promised not to sell medium-range ballistic missiles to Middle East countries, but this was widely seen as no more than a repetition of previous promises. By late February, President Bush personally expressed disappointment with China's response.[6]

It was also clear that changes in both international and domestic politics had restricted the president's flexibility in foreign affairs in general and toward China in particular. He would have much greater difficulty than previous presidents in arguing for secret diplomacy, special treatment, or other exemptions that had marked U.S. treatment of China since Henry Kissinger's secret trip in July 1971.

The American people, media, interest groups, and to a considerable degree, U.S. legislators traditionally place a strong emphasis on morality or values as well as realpolitik or national interest in American foreign policy. The Tiananmen massacre sharply changed American views about China.[7] Instead of pursing policies of political and economic reform, the leaders in Beijing were now widely seen as following policies antithetical to American values and therefore unworthy of American support. Rapidly changing U.S.-Soviet relations also meant that there was no longer a realpolitik or national security rationale of sufficient weight to offset the new revulsion with Beijing's leaders and their repressive policies.

The other side of the world, meanwhile, saw political, economic, and security changes that attracted wide and generally positive attention from the American public, media, interest groups, and legislators. Eastern Europe and the Soviet Union were increasingly following policies of reform in their government structures and economies that seemed to be based on values of individual freedom, political democracy, and economic free enterprise prized in the United States. As a result, these groups tended at times to push U.S. government decisionmakers to be more forthcoming in negotiations and interaction with their East European and Soviet counterparts involving arms control, trade, foreign assistance, and other matters.

The importance of this shift in domestic opinion regarding China and the Soviet bloc countries appeared to be of greater significance than it might have been in the past in determining the course of foreign policy. Since the start of the cold war, the executive branch had been able to argue, on many occasions quite persuasively, that such domestic concerns with common values should not be permitted to override or seriously complicate realpolitik U.S. interests in the protracted struggle and rivalry with the USSR. Now that it was widely seen that the cold war was ending and the Soviet threat was greatly reduced, the ability of the executive branch to control the course of foreign policy seemed to diminish. The administration could no longer argue that the dangers of cold war contention and confrontation required a tightly controlled foreign policy.

In resorting to secret diplomacy in sending Scowcroft and Eagleburger to Beijing, despite the stated administration policy against such contacts, the president and his advisers recognized they were taking a serious risk. The president's actions on China contrasted with his widely applauded efforts to establish himself as a world leader interested in active consultations at home and abroad that would place U.S. policy in line with those of other nations determined to foster world stability and progress. His repeated conferences with European and Japanese leaders after the Tiananmen incident seemed to reflect this pattern, which emerged even more strongly in the president's consideration of U.S. policy in response to Iraq's invasion of Kuwait in August 1990. At home, too, the president made clear that he was interested in consulting widely with Congress in hopes of achieving a bipartisan foreign policy, although his veto of the legislation governing the FSX, a new fighter aircraft for Japan, underlined a parallel determination not to allow Congress to encroach on what he judged were rightful administrative prerogatives in foreign affairs.[8]

According to administration officials, the president clearly hoped that the secret missions would ease the Chinese leaders' sense of isolation in ways that would prevent a further tightening of repression and encourage a return to economic and possibly political reform. The administration, which reportedly did not wish to mislead the American public or U.S. allies, was caught in a dilemma when it announced in June 1989 that it would suspend high-level official contacts with China. One source maintained that at least partly because of ineffective U.S. policy coordination, Secretary of State James Baker pledged to a congressional committee in mid-June that the United States would suspend high-level contacts with the Beijing government as a result of the Tiananmen massacre two weeks earlier. The White House felt bound to repeat this promise, even though it did not favor the policy and was then actively engaged in preparations for the first secret Scowcroft mission of July. The president and his close advisers realized that there could be a serious negative reaction in Congress, the media, and elsewhere at home and abroad once it became known that the president was working secretly to send high-level envoys to China at the same time that the administration publicly was supporting the halt of such contacts as a sanction against Beijing's repressive policies. They judged the risk worth taking, hoping that the secret high-level visit would encourage Beijing to avoid further repression and return to the path of reform.[9] In the event, the Chinese leaders responded only haltingly to U.S. initiatives.

Partisan politics also complicated Bush's ability to sustain a more moderate policy toward China than that demanded by much of the Congress, media, human rights advocates, Chinese students, and other interest groups. Opponents seemed eager to portray the president and his Republican backers as more sympathetic to the "butchers of Beijing" than to Chinese students and other prodemocracy advocates. Ironically, it appeared to be partisan politics that allowed the president to avoid an embarrassing defeat at the hands of the Democratic-controlled Congress, which took up the proposed override of the president's veto of the Chinese immigration measure as its first item of business in January 1990. By arguing for support for the Republican president from wavering Republican senators in the face of a barrage of often-partisan criticism from Democrats, White House lobbyists were able to gain enough votes to sustain the president's veto on January 25, 1990.[10]

The unanticipated defeat of the Democratic leadership's override effort appeared to have a sobering effect. During winter-spring 1990, congressional leaders did not go out of their way to challenge the president's China policy so long as Bush avoided major initiatives or exceptions in dealing with China. In February, the president signed the State Department authorization bill, which contained a version of the sanctions language passed by Congress the previous summer, and the administration delivered a hard-hitting report on conditions in China as part of its annual human rights report to Congress.

Consideration of MFN for China, 1990

Perhaps of more importance, the administration adopted a low public profile on what was expected to be a major issue of controversy—the annual waiver of provisions under the Jackson-Vanik Amendment of the Trade Act. The waiver is required for Chinese goods to receive most-favored-nation tariff treatment by the United States. Loss of MFN would have led to immediate heavy duties on China's then-$12 billion annual exports to the

United States—in effect closing much of the U.S. market to Chinese goods. The last waiver was granted in late May 1989, and the 1990 waiver was due by June 3—coincident with the first anniversary of the Tiananmen demonstrations and crackdown.

Congress, the media, and various human rights groups were widely expected to attack any early administration decision to grant a waiver for China. Under strong political pressure at home and determined to pursue an effective strategy in relations with China, Bush shifted his approach in late winter 1990. He let it be known at home and abroad that he was "disappointed" with the Chinese response to his policy initiatives. He and a small group of aides made clear that the president was reluctant to undertake another major political struggle, like the effort to block the override of the Chinese immigration bill in January 1990, unless Beijing showed its interest in improved U.S.-Chinese relations by easing political repression and releasing dissidents. Thus, the administration was in effect saying to the Chinese government that unless Beijing took some positive steps, the administration might be inclined to avoid controversy by holding back on granting another annual waiver for MFN treatment of Chinese exports to the United States. To be sure that the message got across effectively and clearly to the Chinese leaders, the president and his White House aides made certain that others in the administration did not speak out on this issue until the president announced his decision, at the last minute, to grant another annual waiver for China.[11] The waiver came at a time of several important Chinese gestures to the West, notably allowing the release of dissident Fang Lizhi from the U.S. embassy. This seemed to vindicate the administration's tactics. Facing a possible loss of valuable trading privileges in the United States, the Chinese leaders finally took significant steps to reciprocate the earlier U.S. gestures and to encourage a more constructive atmosphere in U.S.-China relations.[12]

Whether by design or good fortune, the tight White House-controlled restrictions on administration statements regarding MFN in 1990 also had a positive effect within the United States as far as the administration was concerned. It forced Congress, the media, and interest groups to address the issue more practically and directly on its merits. By adopting a low posture, the administration provided less opportunity for those U.S. critics who wished to use the MFN issue in a larger context as a symbol of American support or opposition to the government in Beijing. In the event, many critics of Bush administration policy toward China, after deliberations, came out in favor of granting, with appropriate conditions, MFN treatment for Chinese exports.[13] As a result, in mid-1990 it appeared that the administration's decision to grant a waiver for China—announced finally on May 24—would not be stopped by congressional action. In any event, the House eventually passed bills halting or conditioning MFN for China, but they had little substantive effect given the Senate's refusal to address the issue so late in the session.

Broadening, Deepening Policy Debate, 1991-1992

Over the next two years, the debate between the Bush administration and its congressional backers, on one side, and a large bipartisan group of critics in Congress, on the other, over U.S. policy toward China went through three general stages. The debate duly reflected the broad range of feelings among various organized groups about U.S. China policy.

The first stage saw congressional criticism of China, and of Bush administration policy toward China, moderate in late 1990 and early 1991. This easing reflected U.S. preoccupation with the confrontation with Iraq and the perceived need for China's support in that effort. Behind the scenes, a large group of congressional critics, backed by U.S. groups and interests strongly opposed to Chinese government policies and practices, remained deeply frustrated with Chinese actions. These included the handling of human rights issues since the Tiananmen incident; new evidence of often unscrupulous, unsavory, and arguably irresponsible Chinese practices in trade with the United States, and sales of Chinese missiles and nuclear weapons-related technology. Congressional frustration also focused on the Bush administration's insistence on a continued active and engaged U.S. policy toward Beijing.

The second stage emerged in March-April 1991. There was an outpouring of congressional criticism toward China on human rights, trade, and arms proliferation issues and toward the Bush administration for its "failed" China policy. This was backed by widespread negative media coverage of China and numerous releases of studies and information by interest groups critical of Chinese government policies and behavior. Concerned that congressional anger might jeopardize the annual waiver continuing MFN treatment for Chinese imports (widely seen as the linchpin of the administration "engaged" China policy), and reflecting their own frustrations with China's actions, Bush administration officials toughened U.S. policy in several areas. Most congressional critics persisted with efforts to place firm legislated conditions on MFN for China. However, enough senators were in accord with the president's selectively toughened approach to China, along with unimpeded MFN, to ensure sufficient support to sustain a presidential veto of any legislated conditions on MFN for China.

The third stage came after critical votes on conditional MFN legislation in July 1991. The House vote was heavily against administration policy. In the Senate, forty-four senators, including several farm-state

Democrats, voted with the Bush administration against placing firm conditions on MFN for China. Subsequently, congressional critics kept up a steady drumbeat of attacks on Chinese practices and passed several pieces of legislation critical of China and the administration's policy. Yet they seemed unable to make substantial inroads among those senators who supported the Bush administration's stance assuring continued MFN trade treatment. The Senate adjourned without voting on the House-passed conference bill placing firm conditions on MFN for China.

Over the next year, debate continued along the same lines. It was made more contentious on account of broad U.S. frustration with China's practices and the perceived "soft" policy of Bush. The 1992 election campaign substantially added to the rancor, although the president was able to sustain his vetoes of tough congressional mandates affecting MFN by means of support from a bipartisan group of farm-state senators.

Moderating Debate Prior to the 1991 Crisis

In early 1991 the debate in Congress over China policy was more moderate than at any time since the June 1989 Tiananmen incident. Signs of moderating U.S. criticism of China policy during the last half of 1990 and early 1991 included the relatively mild criticism greeting the Bush administration's acquiescence to Japan's decision in July 1990 to resume its multibillion-dollar aid program to China, which had been suspended after the Tiananmen incident; the fact that Fang Lizhi was allowed to leave after he had spent a year in the U.S. embassy for fear of being arrested; and praise by the administration and some in Congress for the efforts of the five permanent members of the UN Security Council, including China, in reaching a peace plan for Cambodia in August 1990. Most important, Iraq's August 1990 invasion of Kuwait focused U.S. attention on the U.N. Security Council, where China's veto power loomed large in American calculations to obtain support for resolutions condemning the invasion and allowing the use of force to expel Iraq's forces from Kuwait.[14]

Against this backdrop, Foreign Minister Qian Qichen resumed de facto high-level Chinese-American diplomatic contacts in Washington (suspended after Tiananmen) when he traveled there for meetings with President Bush, Secretary of State Baker, and members of Congress in November 1990. According to several sources, congressional members were more cordial in greeting the Chinese minister than was the president, who was said to have included differences in human rights questions among other issues he raised.[15]

Meanwhile, Sino-American trade continued to grow during this period, although many of the economic sanctions adopted by the United States against China in 1989 remained in effect. China was ineligible for investment guarantees through the Overseas Private Investment Corporation (OPIC) or for concessionary trade financing through the Trade Development Program (TDP). A nuclear cooperation program and the process for liberalizing U.S. controls on technology transfer remained frozen. Past routine bilateral high-level economic and commercial policy meetings as well as military exchanges were not resumed.

The Bush administration did renew China's eligibility for Export-Import Bank financing and granted a waiver permitting China to launch an American-made satellite on Chinese rockets.[16] American tourism and investment in China recovered slowly from the sharp drop in the period after June 1989. Sino-American cultural relations followed a similar pattern. Most formal programs that had been suspended by the United States were restored, although some were operating at a lower level than they might have in the absence of the Tiananmen massacre.[17] Public opinion in the United States remained ambivalent about China, although half of those surveyed in some polls favored improved relations with China.[18]

Incremental Change amid Mixed Signals

On the whole, developments in China from 1989 to early 1991 did little to improve prospects for Sino-U.S. relations significantly. Politically, the party and government leadership of China remained at an impasse over a variety of sensitive policy issues, belying an appearance of calm. Central leaders managing day-to-day affairs were hesitant or unable to show much initiative or vision regarding China's future course—a pattern reflecting the conflicting opinions held by the ostensibly retired senior leaders who still wielded formidable power and influence. In one view, the central officials were marking time, waiting for the seemingly inevitable competition for power and political shakeup that would occur once the octogenarian senior leader Deng Xiaoping and his contemporaries passed from the scene. In the meantime, a consensus in support of stability caused Chinese leaders to postpone dealing with the case of the disgraced party chairman Zhao Ziyang, to avoid major leadership shifts, and to be certain that needed new appointments to the central leadership reflected a careful balance of the conservative and reformist views that continued to be at loggerheads in Beijing.[19]

Similarly, the handling of dissidents arrested after the Tiananmen crackdown also reflected a muddled picture resulting from conflicting reformist and conservative trends. While Fang Lizhi was allowed to leave the U.S. Embassy for exile abroad, others were tried in court proceedings in early 1991, coincident with the diversion of world attention to the Persian

Gulf War. Some were treated leniently, according to Chinese spokespeople; but some received sentences of over ten years.[20]

The Chinese military achieved new prominence and gained a greater share of government resources, but its leaders were divided over the appropriate role of the army. The results of the Persian Gulf War underlined the importance of technology in the modern battlefield and reinforced those Chinese military leaders who warned that Maoist-oriented traditions in the army caused China to fall increasingly further behind in international security matters. Some in the military and other conservatives attempted—with little apparent effect—to use a revival of Maoist orthodoxy to counter the ideological debacle caused by the Tiananmen massacre and worldwide decline of authoritarian Marxist regimes.

The weak and divided central government was unable to control some of the social and economic changes affecting coastal regions and other parts of China in close contact with the rest of the world. Dependent on revenue coming from these areas and judging that the "open door" to outside economic, technical, and other exchanges was essential to China's future, even conservative central leaders were forced to modify earlier efforts to restore centralized economic controls and to allow economic reforms to continue at varying paces. The primary emphasis on stability also caused central leaders to opt for an economic program of sustaining moderate growth, while emphasizing attention to the inefficient state industrial sector, which served as a serious impediment to growth and a major source of wasted government expenditure.

The Chinese had more success in dealing with countries around their periphery in Asia.[21] In general, Asian neighbors pragmatically assessed China's size, strategic location, certain comparative economic advantages, and its leadership's desire to avoid additional problems abroad at a time of protracted domestic difficulties. They viewed the Chinese crackdown after Tiananmen more as a symptom of a long-repressive Chinese political system with which they must nonetheless deal, rather than a major turning point in Chinese behavior requiring strong countermeasures. Thus, they were inclined to respond in kind to China's overtures for good relations.

International financial institutions also took a pragmatic view, seeing Beijing's continued economic reform efforts, its willingness and ability to pay off debts, and its open-door economic policies as encouraging signs warranting outside support. China's seat on the U.N. Security Council gave Beijing a major forum in which to play a constructive or at least neutral role on major international issues involving the Persian Gulf War and the conflict in Cambodia—developments that underscored the need to resume high-level political exchanges with China.

Despite the progress, Beijing's leaders showed considerable concern about foreign affairs. In particular, China had worked for many years to establish an important role in the Persian Gulf, not only as an arms supplier but also as the only major power having good relations with all major contending parties in the region. Although Chinese diplomats attempted to salvage an independent role for China during the Persian Gulf confrontation of 1990-1991, China's role and importance were pushed aside by the flow of events dominated by the U.S.-led international coalition. The U.S. success and the concurrent rapid decline of Soviet power and influence in world affairs were also sources of a broader Chinese concern about how the United States would use its newly apparent power. Some in China urged Beijing to work closely with other states to balance America's enhanced power, while others judged that the United States would use its power to interfere in Chinese affairs and to press for political and economic change in China. Amid the fears of American "hegemonism" and "power politics," it was not surprising that Beijing showed few signs of taking substantial initiatives to improve U.S.-China relations.[22]

Crisis over MFN, 1991

In retrospect, moderation in the U.S. debate over China policy in 1990 and early 1991 represented an interlude, caused mainly by U.S. preoccupation with the Persian Gulf War. A loose bipartisan coalition of congressional critics of the administration's policy remained strongly dissatisfied with the administration's posture—which had been unable to demonstrate any major change in Chinese government behavior on sensitive human rights issues. The early months of 1991 brought evidence of new issues involving economic relations and arms proliferation questions, which added to congressional criticism and frustration. Heavy negative media coverage of Chinese actions in these areas, plus activities of U.S. groups critical of China, added to the negative atmosphere in U.S.-China relations. In response, the administration toughened its policy on a variety of human rights, trade, and arms proliferation questions while arguing for continuation of MFN trade status as a centerpiece for continued U.S. engagement with the Beijing leaders. In contrast, congressional critics targeted MFN as a substantial benefit to China that should be made contingent on Chinese behavior regarding sensitive human rights, trade, and arms proliferation questions.[23]

In late winter and spring 1991, Congress resumed attention to other international issues—including China policy—following several months of intense U.S. preoccupation with developments in the confrontation with Iraq over Kuwait. It found that human rights conditions in China had not markedly improved, while new evidence of China's trade and arms proliferation policies fueled congressional determination to force a change in the Bush administration's China policy.[24] Congressional critics were encouraged by various human rights organizations, labor groups concerned with Chinese trade practices, and groups concerned with the spread of weapons of mass destruction and related technology and delivery systems.

In general, a majority in Congress was deeply frustrated both with Chinese government practices and with Bush administration policy, which seemed to many unduly moderate toward the Beijing leaders. This sense of frustration led many in Congress to focus anew on issues associated with the president's annual waiver granting MFN treatment to Chinese imports. Continued MFN was seen to be of central importance to Chinese leaders, who were keenly concerned with promoting Chinese exports and earning hard currency, and to President Bush, who saw it as the linchpin in his policy of continued engagement with China.

Inasmuch as the extension of the MFN waiver was due to be announced in late spring, congressional critics backed by interested organized groups moved to strengthen their case with carefully timed meetings, hearings, press releases, and other actions designed to press both China and the Bush administration to change. Their efforts were also strengthened by continued Chinese government policies and practices seen as inimical to U.S. interests and by a steady stream of press and media reports giving new and often lurid details of Chinese behavior contrary to American interests.

Although it would be inaccurate to characterize the 1991 debate over MFN and other issues in U.S.-China policy as simply partisan, and many congressional Republicans joined in the criticisms of China and Bush administration policy, there was a strong partisan element in the debate. According to interviews with Democratic staff members, some Democrats in Congress were eager to exploit President Bush's and the Republican Party's perceived vulnerabilities over China policy. Following the president's triumph in the Persian Gulf War, China policy seemed to provide a good target to show the perceived poor judgment of the administration and its approach to foreign affairs.[25]

Meanwhile, officials in the Bush administration were not immune from the widespread sense of U.S. frustration with Chinese policy. As Beijing moved inconsistently or not at all in policy areas important to American interests such as human rights, trade policy, and arms proliferation, administration officials were more prone to push for tougher U.S. policies to prompt change in Chinese behavior.[26] In general, such pressure stopped short of jeopardizing MFN treatment for Chinese imports.

The Bush Administration Toughens

The Bush administration was aware in March and early April 1991 that congressional frustration with China's practices would force adjustments in U.S. policy if the administration wanted to avoid congressionally mandated restrictions on MFN tariff treatment for Chinese imports.[27] Administration officials were also becoming increasingly convinced about the need for firmer U.S. policy actions to deal with offensive Chinese policies and practices. The administration was widely expected to grant another annual waiver giving MFN treatment to China—a stance affirmed by the president on May 15.[28] In a May 27 speech at his alma mater, Yale University, the president sought to explain the practical and moral reasoning that lay behind his efforts to keep the MFN status as a key element in U.S. engagement with China, a "catalyst for positive change."[29]

At Yale, President Bush reviewed some of the practical consequences of withdrawal of MFN: it was expected to disrupt seriously Hong Kong's economy and the economically progressive, export-oriented enterprises in south China, and it was likely to lead to Chinese retaliation, cutting off markets for U.S. farm products, aircraft, and other goods. The president also endeavored to seek the moral high ground in the debate, arguing that Americans needed to show faith in their belief in the strength of democratic ideas. By using trade and other contacts fostered by MFN treatment, he said, U.S. policy would be able to cultivate contacts with the Chinese people, promote advantageous commerce, and create a climate for democratic change. "No nation on earth has discovered a way to import the world's goods and services while stopping foreign ideas at the border," he said.[30]

The president and his administration were also careful to buttress such rhetoric with a series of initiatives designed to meet frustrations over Chinese practices in particular areas, while preserving Chinese MFN status. As stated by Secretary Baker in a June 14, 1991, letter to House Speaker Thomas Foley, the administration was endeavoring to use "selective application" of "existing legal mechanisms" to "specific issues of concern" in order to gain results desired by many in Congress. Baker argued that denying MFN to China would destroy "our dialogue" with the Chinese and "dismantle our leverage."[31]

Congress Presses for Conditions on MFN

Despite the administration's initiatives, a broad bipartisan group of critics in the House and Senate—backed by a coalition of human rights, labor, and arms control groups—argued that renewal of MFN for China, widely seen as perhaps the most tangible of U.S. benefits for China, must be made conditional on the Chinese government's behavior on human rights, trade, and proliferation questions. Congress's frustration with the lack of progress or apparent negative trends in Chinese behavior in these areas led to the passage in the House of the United States-China Act of 1991 (H.R. 2212) in a vote of 313 to 112 on July 12, 1991. Sponsored by Rep. Nancy Pelosi, the bill would have required that China, to receive MFN treatment in 1992, must account for and release demonstrators arrested as a result of the Tiananmen incident, end coerced abortion or sterilization, stop exporting ballistic missiles and nuclear technology, and take steps to stop the export of goods to the United States made with prison labor.

The lopsided House vote reflected in part an administration decision to focus its efforts in lobbying against a concurrent Senate measure, sponsored by Majority Leader George Mitchell (S. 1367). That bill required that to receive MFN in 1992 China must provide an accounting of and release demonstrators arrested during the Tiananmen incident; cease exporting prison-made goods to the United States; cease military assistance to the Khmer Rouge in Cambodia; and adhere to agreed-upon principles governing Hong Kong. Other conditions in S. 1367 related to missile sales to the Middle East, adherence to nuclear, chemical, and biological arms control measures, protection of U.S. intellectual property rights, and lowering of Chinese tariff and nontariff barriers to U.S. goods.

Administration efforts were unable to stop the bill, which passed the Senate by a 55-44 vote on July 23, 1991. The vote was widely seen, however, as a solid indication that the administration had enough support in the Senate to sustain an expected presidential veto.[32]

Senate Democrats for MFN

Seven Democratic senators representing farm states with important trade interests with China voted against the Mitchell bill. They were led by Sen. Max Baucus of Montana, who, along with a bipartisan group of fifteen senators, had written Bush a letter on June 19, expressing support for efforts to encourage change in sensitive Chinese policies and belief that withdrawal of MFN represented the "wrong tool for the job." President Bush replied on July 19 enumerating the various initiatives taken by the administration to press for change in China's human rights, arms proliferation, and trade policies.

Senator Baucus was forthright in articulating his opposition to withdrawal of MFN for China. His views supported those of the administration, which argued that withdrawing MFN was too blunt an instrument with too many negative consequences for U.S. interests. He argued for a "smart weapons" approach of tougher U.S. actions focused on specific problem areas. In drawing up the bipartisan letter for the president in June, the senator and his staff worked closely with like-minded senators and their staffs to secure administration assurances that the tougher measures and other policy changes asked for would be forthcoming. These assurances involved reported intensive consultation within the administration on whether or not to pursue so-called 301 trade cases with China and to support Taiwan's entry into the Generalized Agreement on Tariffs and Trade (GATT)—issues suggested by the senators but controversial within the administration. In the event, the senators were sufficiently reassured to go forward with their letter on June 19 and received a generally satisfactory administration reply on July 19—a few days before the Senate voted on S. 1367 on July 23, 1991.[33]

The farm-state senators provided a veto-proof margin on the MFN debate in 1991. Throughout the rest of the year, the debate waxed and waned, but opponents in Congress refrained from completing action on the measure because they knew they did not have the votes in the Senate to override a presidential veto. Strong informal pressure was exerted by the Senate Democratic leadership on the farm-state senators to come into line with other Democrats on this question, but all sides sustained cordial formal working relations.[34]

Behind the leanings of Senator Baucus and his associates lay the targeted lobbying effort of the American grain industry. Recognizing well in advance that U.S. grain sales to China were in some jeopardy as a result of a possible congressional vote conditioning MFN for China, the grain industry focused its efforts on the Senate, where members from grain-producing states provided the margin allowing Bush to continue MFN treatment for China.

The policy standoff between the president and Congress deepened in 1992. The focal points of the debate were the same three key issues of human rights, trade, and weapons proliferation.

Persisting in efforts to preserve a basis for constructive Sino-American relations, notably the important trade relationship supported by U.S. MFN treatment, Bush followed through with some tougher policies toward China. These included the initiation of several trade-related investigations into China's alleged unfair trade practices and violations of intellectual property rights; the seizure of Chinese textile products that had been shipped to the United States in violation of China's textile quotas; and negotiations concerning China's prison labor practices. By such actions, the president tried to assuage critics of China's policies and his administration's "soft" approach toward China, while maintaining sufficient support in Congress and the country for continuing MFN and the U.S.-China economic relationship.

From a tactical point of view, the president was successful in preserving MFN. During the year, Congress acted on three separate bills related to China's normal MFN status. Two were approved in both houses and would have placed conditions on China's MFN status beginning in 1994; these were both vetoed by President Bush, with the vetoes sustained in the Senate. The third measure would have disapproved the president's recommendation to extend MFN to China; this initiative did not pass. As in 1991, the critical margin of difference in the Senate was provided by the bipartisan group of senators concerned with grain exports to China.

Strategically, the president suffered great losses. He was depicted in the media, in congressional debates, and elsewhere as on the defensive in the face of often-strident U.S. advocacy groups and relatively unmoving PRC officials. His actions to assuage U.S. criticism were often seen as too little and too late to deflect congressional, media, and other frustration with the president's approach to China over the previous three years.

Adding fuel to the debate was the 1992 presidential election. As the year wore on, Bush appeared increasingly vulnerable in his re-election bid; the growing popularity of Ross Perot and Bill Clinton, coupled with Clinton's campaign statements that he supported a China policy much tougher than Bush's, put strong political pressure on the incumbent. It also reduced the incentive of the Democratic-controlled Congress to come to an accommodation with the Bush administration over China policy issues. Indeed, seeking partisan advantage prompted some Democrats to strike out in a variety of directions in order to discredit Bush's China policy. This not only supported the continued assaults on MFN, but it was also a factor behind congressional initiatives to pass legislation prescribing certain U.S. policy positions on Hong Kong and permitting Chinese students in the United States to convert to permanent resident status. Congress also considered legislation relating to the establishment of a surrogate broadcasting service comparable to Radio Free Europe in Asia and China. In addition, Congress continued to examine and consider legislation on other issues, such as China's weapons proliferation, trade practices, and human rights abuses.

Notes

1. For background see Robert Sutter, "American Policy toward Beijing," *Journal of Northeast Asian Studies* (winter 1990): 3-14.
2. Information based on interviews with senior-level Bush administration officials and discussed in Robert Sutter, "American Policy toward Beijing."
3. The president's and the administration's actions and congressional and other responses can be monitored in *Congressional Quarterly Weekly Report*, 1989-1990.

4. See *Weekly Compilation of Presidential Documents,* The White House (Washington, D.C., 1989), 238-39; 246-50; 291; 403.

5. See *New York Times* and *Washington Post* coverage of the president's February 1989 visit.

6. See the review of U.S. policy toward China in *Washington Post*, March 7, 1990.

7. See discussion of this issue in *Crisis in China: Prospects for U.S. Policy*, report of the Thirtieth Strategy for Peace, U.S. Foreign Policy Conference, The Stanley Foundation, October 19-21, 1989.

8. See the assessment in *Congressional Quarterly Weekly Report* (February 18, 1989): 332-37.

9. Interview, Washington, November 20, 1990.

10. Discussed in *National Journal* (February 24, 1990): 445-49.

11. This episode, and the incident in June 1989 concerning Secretary Baker's pledge regarding a ban on U.S. high-level visits at the time when the White House was secretly planning the first Scowcroft visit, raise questions about the State Department's importance in U.S. China policy at this juncture. In addition, senior State Department officers at the U.S. Embassy in Beijing claimed no knowledge of the Scowcroft visit on the day after Scowcroft departed from Beijing in December 1989. They referred all queries to Ambassador Lilley (interview, Beijing; December 11, 1989). At least some State Department officials judged that the department's staff work on China policy was not influential in guiding China policy during the Bush administration, except insofar as their efforts came to the attention of such senior leaders as Secretary of State Baker. Because of close personal ties with the president, Secretary Baker was seen to have the ability to insert himself into the policy process if he chose. Baker was considered influential in charting the course of U.S. foreign policy in a number of areas, but his influence on China policy was not readily apparent, for it was overshadowed by the president's strong personal views and insistence on playing a direct role in managing U.S.-China relations (interview, Washington, November 21, 1990).

12. Interviews, Washington, November 20-21, 1990.

13. Winston Lord, "Bush's Second Chance on China," *New York Times*, May 9, 1990.

14. For background, see *Current History* (September 1991): 248-49. In the event, China did not veto the use of force against Iraq's occupation of Kuwait.

15. Interviews, Washington, D.C., April 1991, December 1991, and January 1992.

16. The CRS issue briefs 84135 and 92022 provide a good summary of U.S. sanctions against China.

17. For background, see *New York Times*, November 6, 1991.

18. See John E. Reilly, ed., *American Public Opinion and U.S. Foreign Policy in 1991* (Chicago: Chicago Council on Foreign Relations, 1991), 24.

19. See, among others, U.S. Congress, Joint Economic Committee, *China's Economic Dilemmas in the 1990s*, vols. I and II (Washington, D.C.: U.S. Government Printing Office, 1991). The articles provide very useful overviews of Chinese politics, military trends, economic policies, and other issues.

20. See, for example, *New York Times*, January 6, 1991, 3.

21. See, among others, John Garver, "Chinese Foreign Policy: The Diplomacy of Damage Control," *Current History* (September 1991): 241-46.

22. See Robert Sutter, *China's View of the New World Order—Possible Implications for Sino-U.S. Relations*, CRS Report 91-665 F, September 11, 1991, 6.

23. All parties in the U.S.-China policy debate recognized that Congress had influence over U.S.-China policy through its ability to shape U.S. MFN policy. Chinese and Bush administration leaders were aware that Congress had the option to block the granting of MFN or to pass new legislation that would place firm conditions on future granting of MFN for China. For an overview of the crisis see *Current History* (September 1991): 249-50. For weekly coverage, see *Congressional Quarterly Weekly Report.*

24. See notably *Congressional Quarterly Weekly Report* (April 27, 1991): 1044-46.

25. Interviews, Washington, D.C., December 1991.

26. Interviews, Washington, D.C., December 1991.

27. Interviews, Washington, D.C., April 4, 1991.

28. The president's formal message on MFN for China came on May 29.

29. The president's May 29 message is seen in U.S. Department of State *Dispatch,* June 17, 1991, 430; his speech at Yale is seen in *Congressional Quarterly Weekly Report,* 1459-60.

30. President's message, *Congressional Quarterly Weekly Report,* 1459-60.

31. Letter from Secretary of State Baker to Speaker of the House Foley, June 14, 1991.

32. The House and Senate votes are reviewed in *Congressional Quarterly Weekly Report,* (July 27, 1991): 2053-56.

33. Interviews, Washington, D.C., December 1991. A precedent influencing Senator Baucus's decision to send the letter and the administration's response was provided by congressional-administration handling a few weeks earlier of the so-called "fast-track" procedures for trade agreements, such as the North American Free Trade Agreement and the Uruguay Round of the Generalized Agreement on Tariffs and Trade (GATT). In the debate leading up to the congressional vote on May 23 reauthorizing expedited "fast-track" consideration of such trade accords, several congressional members sent a letter to the administration articulating concerns they felt would have to be met before they would support reauthorizing fast-track procedures. Administration spokesmen responded a few days before the vote, laying out how they planned to meet the congressional concerns. Congressional staff interviewed in December 1991 highlighted the importance of the precedent of the congressional-administration exchange on fast track procedures.

34. Interviews with congressional staff concerned indicated that there was strong feeling among some Democratic staff officials over Senator Baucus's stance on the China MFN issue.

Chapter 4

The MFN Debate during the Clinton Administration

Overview

During the 1992 presidential campaign, the Democratic candidate, Bill Clinton, supported the position of prominent congressional Democratic leaders and others that conditions should be placed on the annual renewal of China's MFN benefits. In a sign of the future direction of his China policy, the new president appointed former U.S. Ambassador to China Winston Lord, a leading critic of Bush administration policies and one of the earliest proponents of MFN conditionality, as his assistant secretary of state for East Asia and the Pacific.[1]

In the spring of 1993, the new Clinton administration began drafting a new executive order—one that would for the first time renew MFN with the sorts of conditions proposed by Congress, but never enacted, under Bush. According to the analysis of Jim Mann, corroborated by discussion at the American Assembly Study Group, this process changed the focus for outside advocacy groups.[2] For the first time since the MFN debate began, their efforts came to be directed more at the executive branch than at Congress. Hong Kong Governor Chris Patten and the Dalai Lama went to the new Clinton White House—the former urging an unconditional extension of MFN, the latter dramatizing the case for inclusion of strong language protecting Tibet. Less-prominent individuals and constituencies had fewer opportunities to make their views known to the administration. The drafting of the administration's executive order, carried out by Lord, was done largely in private. The focus of the discussions was between Lord (representing the administration) and Senator Mitchell and Representative Pelosi (representing Capitol Hill forces in favor of MFN conditionality). The Chinese government was also quietly consulted, both in private meetings between Secretary of State Warren Christopher and the Chinese ambassador to Washington, and during a visit by Lord to China. Outside interests, notably the American business community, had little involvement in the drafting of the executive order. Within the new administration, economic agencies like the Commerce Department and the new National Economic Council remained at a distance.

The administration assumed that China could meet, and would be willing to meet, the terms of the executive order. Over the previous three years, a sort of informal conditionality had developed between the Bush team and Beijing: in an effort to head off congressional action on MFN, China had, on its own, made various concessions, such as the well-timed releases of some dissidents. By this time, however, the situation in China had changed, and with that change came a decidedly more assertive and active U.S. business lobby working for secure MFN for China.

In early 1992, China altered its economic policies. Following a visit by Deng Xiaoping to southern China, the government opened the way for a dramatic increase in economic growth. In effect, China abandoned the policies fostered by Premier Li Peng of holding down China's rate of growth to guard against inflation. In the wake of Deng's decision, China achieved startling rates of growth of about 12 to 13 percent in 1993-1994.[3]

This change in policy was probably motivated by domestic concerns; it also had important ramifications for foreign investors, for foreign governments, and thus, indirectly, for the dynamics of the MFN debate in the United States. Over the next two years, top Fortune 500 companies, such as AT&T, led the fight for unconditional renewal of China's MFN benefits. American companies now saw China as the world's fastest-growing big market, one in which government policies, law, and practice could support rational investment, and consequently, a market evolving to one of the main emphases in their international business strategies. No longer would the business constituency for MFN be confined mostly, as it had been up at that time, to American importers and grain exporters.

From the negotiations among Lord, Mitchell, and Pelosi came a compromise. The new administration would confine the conditions for MFN renewal to human rights plus the usual Jackson-Vanik freedom of immigration requirement; it would leave the issues of weapons proliferation and trade, which had been included in recent versions of the congressional MFN legislation, to be handled through "other tools."[4] Clinton's human rights conditions were considerably less stringent than they had been in the proposed congressional legislation. Instead of requiring China to release dissidents and provide an accounting of political prisoners in its jails, the executive order required "overall significant progress" on human rights over the course of the year.

To human rights groups, the administration argued that the executive order went further than Bush ever had, noting it was the first time any administration had imposed additional conditions other than Jackson-Vanik on renewing MFN. To those on the other side of the MFN debate, the administration suggested that the executive order was aimed at coopting Congress and thus moving to bring an end to the controversy.[5]

A year later, U.S. business executives and officials in the economic agencies of the Clinton administration complained that they had little involvement in the drafting of the executive order. In fact, if they were not involved, it was in part because they did not realize until far later how much China would turn the executive order into a frontal challenge to American business. At the time, they seemed to accept the administration's view that it was imposing conditions China could satisfy, and that the new order was a way of reducing, rather than exacerbating, the tensions over MFN.[6]

Nevertheless, politically important U.S. business interests began weighing in against a punitive U.S.-China policy, as disclosed by *Los Angeles Times* columnist Jim Mann.[7] In August 1993, the Clinton administration imposed sanctions, required by U.S. law, on the sale of satellite equipment to China in retaliation for the Chinese sale of M-11 missile components to Pakistan. The Bush administration had earlier imposed sanctions on sales of satellite parts to China under the same provision; this was, in fact, one of the "other tools" often proposed as an alternative to MFN.

The satellite sanctions hit a couple of American companies, including the Hughes Aircraft Company, hard; Hughes's chairman, C. Michael Armstrong, was one of Clinton's leading supporters within the American business community in the 1992 campaign. Like other firms in the U.S. defense industry, Hughes was grappling with cutbacks in the Pentagon and intelligence budgets. As was the case with other defense firms, a significant portion of Hughes's American manufacturing was situated in California, whose electoral votes were crucial to Clinton's past and future in the White House.

Armstrong fought the satellite sanctions both privately and in public. He wrote a private letter to Clinton, reminding the president of his past support and suggesting it might not be there in the future. The sanctions could cost Hughes alone a billion dollars in business and 4,000 to 5,000 jobs, he said. "It escapes me what effect our laying off 4,000 to 5,000 more people in California and shifting the export business to Europe has on the Chinese," Armstrong said in one speech.[8]

Such protests caught the attention of Clinton's economic policy team, which had been paying special attention to the recession in California. They backed efforts evident by early autumn 1993, whereby the administration undertook the first full-scale review of its China policy, announcing a new policy of high-level engagement with Chinese leaders. As part of that engagement, the administration agreed that Clinton would hold his first meeting with Chinese President Jiang Zemin during an Asia Pacific Economic Cooperation (APEC) economic summit meeting of Asia and Pacific leaders in Seattle.

Increasingly, leaders in the Clinton administration concerned with economic issues and relations with business began to express reservations both privately and publicly about the wisdom of the MFN executive order. In the process, they diminished the credibility of the administration's position in the eyes of the Chinese government.[9]

By the time the secretary of state visited Beijing in March 1994, the Chinese government was confident that it could ignore and, indeed, defy the U.S. requests for human rights improvements (by detaining dissidents both before and during his visit) without serious consequences.[10] To some observers Christopher represented merely one wing of the U.S. government, rather than the Clinton administration as a whole.

At this time, U.S. advocates with an interest in the MFN issue focused on influencing the Clinton administration—although, as an indirect means of doing so, organizations regularly lobbied Congress and the press as well.[11] By early May, nearly 800 American companies and trade associations wrote letters to Clinton. Besieged by requests from business representatives, pro-business members of Congress issued press releases and made floor speeches in support of MFN extension; congressional human rights supporters like Mitchell and Pelosi responded in kind.[12]

Some business advocates pushed for more than annual renewal of MFN for China; they wanted to end the debate with a one-time approval. Human rights groups sometimes gave ground in the face of the heavy business assault. Officials of Human Rights Watch/Asia proposed increasing the duties on Chinese goods by only a relatively small percentage, rather than simply removing MFN benefits and letting the tariffs hike up to the sometimes prohibitive levels of goods without MFN. Many others, such as China's exiled democracy advocate, Fang Lizhi, called for revocation of MFN benefits for goods from state industries only, continuing the benefits for goods made by private or quasi-private entities. Organized labor pressed for special penalties on the products made by Chinese enterprises with links to the People's Liberation Army.

The shift by human rights groups to less-drastic approaches failed to slow the momentum building up within the Clinton administration and Congress for ending MFN conditionality regarding human rights issues. First, the human rights groups' switch toward less-drastic penalties came too late in the process. Second, the groups failed to unify behind a single approach.

Third, the groups differed over their ultimate goals. Some favored condition-ality for its own sake, as a means of achieving progress on the ground in China; they would moderate the penalties in order to preserve the condition-ality. Others saw conditionality as merely a means of winning broader political support for other aims: registering moral disapproval of the Chinese government, undermining the regime, and avoiding any action that would give it a sense of legitimacy. Not eager to moderate the approach, they believed that a tactical retreat would in itself strengthen and convey legitimacy to the Chinese regime. The AFL-CIO's Lane Kirkland, for example, made clear that he favored outright revocation of MFN.[13]

On May 26, 1994, Clinton announced that he had finally decided to "delink" China's MFN status from the human rights conditions he had earlier attached. In the process, he acknowledged that China "continues to commit very serious human rights abuses" and had failed to meet the "overall significant progress" required by the 1993 executive order, but said America's broader strategic interests justified a reversal of the policy. In August, the House decided by a large margin, 280 to 152, to support Clinton's uncondi-tional extension, thus effectively reversing the course it had set on MFN policy in a series of votes dating back to 1990.[14]

The Tug-of-War over MFN during the Clinton Administration, 1993-1994

U.S. policymakers considered a variety of concerns in deciding on U.S. policy over the MFN issue with China.[15] They included broad concerns over long- and short-term strategic interests, economic concerns, and values, as well as the more narrowly defined considerations of constituents and others. Although the U.S. government does not decide policy on the basis of competing lobbies or interest groups, at one level of analysis U.S. policy-making over MFN and China during the 1990s included a tug-of-war between competing interests and advocacy groups. On one side, advocates led by human rights organizations gained prominence in the years after the Tiananmen incident. On the other side, U.S. business groups had an ever-increasing interest in the burgeoning China market. These groups altered their tactics to adjust to changes in the administration or shifts in conditions in China. Their relative influence in U.S. decisionmaking over time provided a useful barometer of U.S. policy leanings. In general, the human rights groups have lost influence in recent years, while business groups have become more important.

In retrospect, it was remarkable that human rights groups were able to exert as much influence as they did over the course of several years. It was a testament to their hard work as well as to the deep and long-lasting

U.S. popular antipathy to the Chinese government, fed by the Tiananmen incident and media coverage of numerous other Chinese government affronts to U.S. interests and values. By contrast, U.S. business interests took longer to become actively mobilized in the China debate after Tiananmen, especially as they tended to rely on President Bush to preserve the fundamental elements of the U.S.-China economic relationship. The election of Bill Clinton and the rising importance of the China market to American businesses sharply increased U.S. business lobbying. Backed by ample resources and concrete evidence of their importance to the constituencies of many congressional members and to the administration, business lobbyists were able to make a stronger case than previously in the debate over MFN.

Of course, these groups were not alone in dealing with China policy. All the many groups listed in the appendix of this study have at one time or another played a role in influencing U.S. policy toward China during this period. The face-off in Washington over China's MFN status in 1993 and 1994, however, appeared to pit business interests against human rights and labor groups in particular, though policymakers certainly considered other factors as well.

Possibly among the most important of other factors influencing the debate at this time was the reported role of campaign contributors, at home and abroad, with an interest in U.S.-China trade and overall U.S.-China relations. The large-scale expenses involved in the U.S. political process make U.S. politicians sensitive to those who provide financial assistance. Such assistance is regulated by federal law. The regulations provide limits on who can give and how much they can give to individual candidates. At the same time candidates also benefit greatly from so-called "soft money," which often dwarfs the amount of money given to individual candidates and is used in broad-based campaigns that assist certain candidates over others. Candidates also benefit from the efforts of many issue-advocacy groups in the United States and abroad.

U.S. citizens with an interest in U.S.-China relations are able to contribute to candidates, to soft money campaigns, and to issue-advocacy groups. Foreign individuals and interests are allowed to support issue-advocacy groups, and also, under certain conditions, can contribute soft money useful in political campaigns.

Media disclosures and congressional inquiries in 1996 and 1997 focused on the reported influence of foreign and domestic sources of political financial support on U.S. policy toward China. It was repeatedly alleged that pro-China business interests, and the Chinese government and Chinese government enterprises, were funneling money—sometimes illegally—into U.S. political campaigns and broader political activities. The thrust of U.S. media coverage gave an impression that such funding was an important factor in determining the change in the Clinton administration's stance on MFN for China in 1994.[16]

It is yet unknown just how important these reported political donations to the U.S.-China policy were. By the end of 1997, the Senate committee investigating these and other reported campaign irregularities finished hearings and prepared a report that provided little concrete evidence that Chinese government contributions or contributions of others with an interest in U.S.-China relations had much of an impact on U.S. China policy. A House committee continued its investigation but with little indication that it could establish with any more certainty connections between donations and China policy.[17] Assessments of available evidence suggest that, regardless of the political campaign contributions, the balance of forces between pro- and anti-MFN forces was such that it mandated the shift toward a more pragmatic U.S. policy toward China.

Critics of MFN for China

Human rights groups trying to influence U.S. policy toward China included Amnesty International USA, Human Rights Watch/Asia, and Freedom House. These groups have neither the financial wherewithal nor the grass-roots backing to employ the conventional tactics of Washington politics: most of their officers are in nonprofit research groups whose tax status precludes obvious, conventional lobbying. What they can do effectively is to ensure that reports and data supporting their cases concerning human rights abuses are aired in the media.

A coalition of Chinese dissident groups, church groups, environmental groups, consumer groups, and the AFL-CIO joined the human rights groups. They include some with a strong "right to life" platform that is at odds with China's record on abortion and other forms of coerced birth control, and others who resent Chinese suppression of religious freedom for Christians and others in China.

The Chinese Dissident Community. Immediately after the Tiananmen Square incident, Chinese dissidents staying in the United States won broad support from members of Congress and the media; they succeeded in getting resolutions introduced and passed in Congress. The International Federation of Chinese Students and Scholars (IFCSS), an organization claiming thousands of members within the United States, soon became the "spokesperson" for the Chinese dissident community in the United States and China. Its representatives appeared frequently before congressional hearings and news shows. Subsequently, the Chinese dissident groups often drifted because of internal bickering and funding problems. By 1994, individual groups like the Laogai Foundation and others continued to have a following on Capitol Hill and elsewhere, but the overall impact of Chinese dissident groups was much reduced.

Organized Labor. A federation of eighty-six unions, the AFL-CIO represents about 75 percent of organized labor in the United States. The federation has an active program critical of China over human rights abuses, especially labor rights and use of prison labor. An important force on the side of those criticizing and urging trade restrictions and sanctions against China, the federation lobbies effectively and influences many executive branch and congressional decisionmakers.

Right to Life, Religious Freedom Groups. The Family Research Council, the Free Congress Foundation, and the U.S. Catholic Conference and other groups with a strong right-to-life platform and strong support for religious freedom have been key critics of China in recent years. Appalled by continued reports of coerced abortion and religious freedom violations in China, they mobilize political support, especially among conservative Republican members of Congress, to stand against MFN for China and to apply other sanctions against the PRC.

Tibet. Groups active in arguing for conditioning MFN for China on human rights grounds have included Tibetan activists led by the International Campaign for Tibet. They notably sponsored visits by the Dalai Lama to Washington, D.C., that served to highlight Chinese repression and human rights abuses in Tibet and to mobilize congressional and administration support for legislation and policies geared to preserving Tibetan freedoms.

Of course, not all groups supporting the conditioning of MFN for China argued on human rights grounds. Advocates concerned with weapons proliferation were especially active in 1991 and 1992. Clinton's executive order of 1993 had the effect of focusing these groups' attention to "other tools" of U.S. policy cited by the president at that time. These focused on using existing legislated sanctions, mainly economic sanctions apart from conditioning MFN, in reaction to Chinese proliferation practices. Meanwhile, some groups strongly supporting U.S. endeavors to improve human rights in China argued against placing conditions on granting MFN treatment for China. Prominent in this regard was a leading Hong Kong democrat, Martin Lee, who came to Washington to urge U.S. decisionmakers to avoid jeopardizing MFN on grounds that such action would seriously upset economic and related human rights conditions in Hong Kong and coastal China.

Weaknesses of the Coalition of Critics of MFN

The Harvard specialist Steven Teles and others have pointed out that the constellation of forces arguing against MFN for China had several weaknesses in terms of relative strategy as well as the cohesion and durability of their policy coalition.[18] In particular, the anti-MFN coalition represented a wide assortment of groups, each of which had a particular reason for opposing MFN, driven by a different world view and often sharply varying ideologies. Although united in its concern with China's human rights behavior, the human rights community is not as united in the vehemence with which it pursues opposition to unconditional MFN. Some human rights and religious groups, such as Amnesty International and the U.S. Catholic Conference, take no official position on MFN. Many of the others support conditional MFN, even though they privately admit to wanting to preserve the trade relationship that MFN makes possible. Even within the community of activists interested in Tibet, for example, there are differences on policy preferences. One Tibetan source told Teles that there is some tension between some of the more radical groups who want revocation and groups in Washington who are more of the philosophy that they should "achieve something."

The labor movement is interested in MFN for somewhat different reasons. The AFL-CIO is in favor of revocation of China's MFN status, and its motivations, depending upon the source, are some amalgam of human rights concerns and preservation of U.S. jobs through trade protections.

Although the human rights groups take a fundamentally agnostic position (or are even supportive) toward U.S. trade with China, the labor movement is opposed, for a set of reasons not substantially different from those at issue in the debate over the North American Free Trade Agreement (NAFTA). Unlike the human rights groups, which have the potential for relatively wide-ranging cooperation with business on non-MFN related issues, this potential for cooperation is not as evident with labor unions, which tend to oppose business on many if not most issues with an economic motivation.

Right-wing ideological organizations appear to have a different set of motivations for interest in China. Although conservative-leaning think tanks, such as the American Enterprise Institute and the Heritage Foundation, are generally supportive of a nonconfrontational relationship with China, some of those further right still retain much of the old cold war distrust of communist regimes. One of the more influential groups in Washington that opposes unconditional MFN is the Family Research Council. The council, along with the Christian Coalition, is seen to be the most important Washington presence of the Christian Right. Other parts of the conservative anti-MFN coalition include the Eagle Forum and Concerned Women for America. The motivation of these groups is similar, focusing primarily on China's one-child policy, forced abortion and sterilization, oppression of Christian groups, and, to some degree, concern about China as a potential strategic threat. Finally, there are groups, such as the U.S. Business and

ʿial Council, that are generally protectionist while supporting
ʾrvative economic policies domestically. Their most prominent supporter
ʾoger Milliken, the textile magnate.

There is little reason for most of these groups to work together on
issues other than MFN. Teles has pointed out that while labor unions
applaud Milliken's opposition to open trading borders, they consider him a
supporter of right-to-work laws. Although conservative groups agree with the
human rights community about China's cavalier approach to fundamental
freedoms, the political backgrounds and overall view of the world of activists
on either side are radically different. Because there are few ongoing links
between the parts of the anti-MFN coalition, and because of the varying
policy preferences and overall agendas of the groups, fusing the parts of the
coalition into a whole is a difficult process.

Business Groups

Business groups concerned with agricultural exports to China, imports
of Chinese toys, shoes, textiles, and consumer goods, and the interests of
Hong Kong have been worried about the future of U.S.-China trade since
the Tiananmen incident.[19] At that time, many business interests were
reluctant to step forward to articulate their views in the face of strongly
negative media coverage of developments in China and negative popular
opinion in the United States. The increasingly serious U.S. domestic
challenge to U.S. MFN, combined with a growing American perception of
the importance of the China market, prompted U.S. business to change its
approach, leading to a marked rise in the efforts and effectiveness of U.S.
business lobbying.[20]

By 1991, large companies and trade groups, such as the Emergency
Committee for American Trade (ECAT) and the U.S.-China Business
Council, had united under one umbrella organization—the Business Coalition
for U.S.-China Trade. A representative of Hong Kong business interests in
Washington and an active member of the Business Coalition for U.S.-China
Trade, R. D. Folsom, characterized the evolution of business lobbying this
way: "In 1990, our base was 10 to 30 companies; CEOs were reluctant to
move forward since no one wanted to be an apologist [for China's behavior
in the Tiananmen Square incident]."[21]

In the meantime, however, China's economy began to grow rapidly and
U.S. business activity in China again began to accelerate. The attitude of
U.S. business toward lobbying quickly changed. "By 1994 and 1995,
companies were almost willing to stake anything," said Folsom. "At the
meetings they kept saying, 'It's bigger here than anywhere else,' and they
kept pointing at future business prospects and market potential in China."[22]

As China continued to evolve commercially and open up to foreign trade and investment, many U.S. companies found themselves driven to the Chinese market by strong competition from other nations. The combination of rising U.S. business activity in China and the very real possibility that MFN would be revoked or conditioned by Congress catalyzed the business lobby effort.

Business Coalition for U.S.-China Trade. In 1991, over seventy-five major trade groups and companies formed the Business Coalition for U.S.-China Trade to help bolster then-President George Bush's stance for unconditional extension of China's MFN.[23] Although there were many trade groups and associations that worked on China-related trade issues, "the Business Coalition was formed in order to provide a single voice for the business community," said the coalition's chairman, Calman Cohen.[24] "The idea was to use a big-tent approach and to involve leading corporations." The membership included the U.S. Chamber of Commerce, ECAT, the 500-member National Foreign Trade Council, the U.S.-China Business Council, law-firm lobbyists, and large companies. "Each group continued to do its own work on trade, but when it came to the MFN issue, we thought it would be more effective if there was only one voice," said Cohen.

The coalition's purpose is to "develop the policy position for the business community," said Cohen. It serves as a forum for trade associations and companies to meet, share ideas, and plan the agenda and lobbying strategies on China-trade issues. "The Coalition is an informal lobby. Its objective is not to be out front," said Folsom.[25]

The coalition reportedly has grown to include over 800 member companies and trade associations, and, according to a 1996 position paper, it had exported over $12 billion in manufactured goods, farm products, and services to China in 1995, supporting over 200,000 high-wage, high-skill U.S. jobs.[26] The composition of the coalition ranges from U.S. multinational corporations to trade associations to port cities and state chambers of commerce, all of whom trade heavily with China. Importers tend to import labor-intensive manufactured goods, while exporters tend to export hi-tech, agricultural, aviation, telecommunications, and transportation goods.

After the 1992 presidential election, when a seemingly anti-MFN candidate was elected president, the coalition changed lobbying strategies and adopted the dual objective of targeting Clinton and the leadership of Congress. Cohen noted that in focusing on the administration, "the most effective way is to speak directly with the president and the senior most people in his administration." The coalition thus began making contacts with President-elect Clinton and his staff to educate them on the MFN issue "before Clinton was even inaugurated," said Cohen. It also continued to spend "far more time with Congress since we have to meet individually with them," he noted.[27]

When targeting Congress, Cohen believed that "it was critical to persuade Congress that U.S. companies in China are creating better working conditions, living standards, and economic rights for Chinese workers and that revoking China's MFN would cut off that process."[28] Part of the congressional strategy was analyzing "how members voted in the past to try and get a sense of the members and find where the possibility is to influence."[29] Folsom noted that business sometimes lobbies all members, especially when there is a key vote on the House or Senate floors. Although lobbyists usually focus on committees, such as the House Ways and Means, the House International Relations, the Senate Foreign Relations, and the Senate Finance Committees, "it quickly goes beyond the committee." Attention then turns toward important individual representatives and senators.

From 1991 to 1992, the coalition focused on the Senate to sustain Bush's veto on conditioning MFN. For example, in 1991, "cowed by staunch opposition in the House to unconditional extension of MFN, footwear retailers focused on garnering enough votes in the Senate."[30] Their strategy changed to targeting the House after the Clinton election. When Clinton ran a campaign on overturning Bush's policy of engagement, "we knew we had to work with the administration," said Cohen. "If Clinton turned the policy around, he needed to have congressional support." In addition, since MFN is a tariff issue, it must originate in the House Ways and Means Committee. So by first targeting the House, the business community had greater chance of preventing the passage of conditional MFN, causing a possible gridlock between the Congress and the administration, and relaunching of MFN onto the headlines.

The Emergency Committee for American Trade (ECAT). ECAT has been a steady, driving force in the efforts to preserve MFN for China. It has a membership of approximately sixty corporate leaders and CEOs of U.S.-owned export groups who "believe in and support measures designed to expand international trade and investment.[31] ECAT was formed in 1967 to lobby against import-quota bills. With the increasing importance of trade issues, it has since become one of the nation's most powerful trade associations and trade watchdog groups.

Calman Cohen has led and directed this group's efforts since 1981.[32] Part of the "organization's clout and authority on trade issues is derived from Cohen's ability to call on the CEOs of many ECAT members to lobby Congress on many issues," said a congressional staff aide.[33]

Under Cohen, ECAT took the lead in organizing business groups during the MFN crisis and in creating the Business Coalition for U.S.-China Trade. ECAT's biggest battles in terms of China have been lobbying for MFN as well as anti-dumping cases, and China's entrance into the World Trade Organization, albeit on ECAT terms, not China's.[34] This business group's lobbying techniques have focused on contacting the president and key members in his administration and Congress, engaging in grass-roots lobbying efforts, and using think tanks and the media to gain favorable public opinion. For example, in 1993 and 1994, they reportedly targeted editorial boards of state newspapers to run letters on MFN, and they also recruited key people to give speeches across the country.[35]

U.S.-China Business Council. Another powerful and vocal group, the U.S.-China Business Council is a "private, non-profit membership association that represents the interests of U.S. business in China."[36] The council, formed in 1973 after President Nixon's visit to the PRC, now has offices in Washington, D.C., and Beijing. While its primary function is to consult and advise companies in China and to serve as a trade and information liaison, it also works as an advocate in Washington for its member companies.

Currently, the council has approximately 285 members and an annual budget of $4 million that comes from membership dues. Its membership overlaps with ECAT's and other trade organizations'.

The council works more with the administration than Congress because the administration has more functionaries in different departments who work on China. "Building relationships within Congress occurs slowly since there is less of a China focus and because changes occur more frequently," said Paul Lamb, the council's program manager.[37]

Although the U.S.-China Business Council works with congressional aides on different committees, Lamb also stated that "our approach is to focus on outreach and to deal individually with Congress." The council does not actively solicit congresspeople, he says "They call us." Lamb also noted that the council does not employ formal lobbying efforts nor does it send lobbyists to the Hill or administration. "The Council only has one full-time lobbyist," said Lamb.

Nonetheless, in a 1995 article in *The China Business Review,* the council's bimonthly magazine, council President Robert Kapp gave a brief synopsis of the organization's lobbying tactics for that year:

> By the third week of July (1995), key Council staff members were 100 percent engaged, mobilizing member companies, strategizing with allies in the business community, meeting with legislators and their staff, writing updates and position papers, and making the case for restraint and sobriety to the media in order to avert a major setback in U.S.-China commercial and diplomatic relations.[38]

Council members also visited congressional representatives from districts where member companies manufacture products for export to China, and they stressed the job and money loss if MFN were revoked or conditioned.[39]

The council also coordinates ongoing programs, such as "China on the Hill," which works with state delegations active in U.S.-China trade. It hosts luncheons and co-hosts seminars and conferences with think tanks to appeal to companies and government officials.

American Chambers of Commerce

Other forces that have lobbied on the MFN issue are the American chambers of commerce in Hong Kong, Taipei, and Beijing. They often send delegations to lobby both Congress and the administration before presidential decisions and congressional votes on the issue. In addition to meetings with members of certain key committees and subcommittees dealing with China trends, the chambers' member companies also put pressure on lawmakers through their home offices.[40]

Hong Kong Groups

Because of Hong Kong's vital role in U.S.-China trade, many groups, public and private, lobby on its behalf. Public groups consist of American and Hong Kong Chambers of Commerce, Hong Kong-hired law firms or consulting groups, and representative offices of the Hong Kong government, such as the Hong Kong Economic and Trade Office (HKETO) in Washington. Hong Kong business- or government-backed delegations, sometimes from the Hong Kong General Chamber of Commerce or Trade Office, lobby Congress and the administration. Large companies active in Hong Kong trade also hire professional lobbyists or maintain a lobby staff within their congressional-affairs department.

According to figures published in the *South China Morning Post,* the Hong Kong government spent $11.6 million on lobbying and public relations in 1993.[41] Some of this money presumably was spent on the several delegations of congressional members and staff members sent to Hong Kong at Hong Kong government expense for week-long orientation trips. Private Hong Kong groups are also sending congressional delegations for such visits. The excursions make congressional decisionmakers more aware of the importance of the MFN decision and other U.S. trade matters with China for Hong Kong's economy and society, and for the broad range of important American interests in Hong Kong.

IIPA

Another business group that lobbies on non-MFN issues in U.S.-China trade is the umbrella group for the entertainment industry, the International Intellectual Property Alliance (IIPA), a coalition of eight trade associations that encompass the music, movie, videogame, software, and book industries.[42] Established in 1984, the IIPA represents over 5 percent of the U.S. economic GDP and provides legal analyses on ways to improve copyright protection and the implementation of such laws in countries all over the world.

Since 1989, the IIPA has provided annual reports to the office of the U.S. Trade Representative (USTR) on intellectual property rights (IPR) issues overseas that affect U.S. companies. Its work is both formal and informal, providing reports to the government, and making frequent visits to foreign countries to assess those countries' IPR situations.

Although the IIPA works primarily with USTR and the Commerce Department, it also works with Congress. According to IIPA Vice-President and General Counsel Maria Strong, IIPA is usually most effective with Congress when it works on amending U.S. trade laws involving international property, WTO, or IPR enforcement overseas.[43] The alliance often testifies before congressional committees, and as of March 1996, it had appeared three times in hearings over the previous eight months.

Chinese Government Efforts

An assessment of the tug-of-war among U.S.- based groups over the MFN issue must include the efforts of the Chinese government and its embassy in Washington, D.C. At a general level, the Chinese government sometimes has appeared to be astute in judging U.S. opinion on the MFN issue. It decided to take a tough line in order to prompt the United States to de-link MFN from human rights concerns during Warren Christopher's April 1994 visit to Beijing. At that time, Chinese officials appeared well aware of the growing importance of the China market to U.S. business interests and understood how those interests could be motivated to influence policy in the administration and Congress. They carefully reminded U.S. business leaders and officials that other developed countries were standing ready to absorb whatever economic opportunities were lost by the United States as a result of a decision to cut off MFN.[44]

The Chinese government also worked through its embassy or through other channels to direct lobbyists or others to influence U.S. government decision-making in favorable ways. Sometimes pro-PRC lobbyists have been seen by seasoned and attentive observers as effective, but more often than not they have been seen—at least until recently—to have had no major bearing on U.S. decision-making.[45]

Seemingly more effective in dealing with Congress have been PRC-backed efforts to sponsor expense-paid trips to China by congressional members and staff. Several delegations go each year under the auspices of such organizations as the U.S. Asia Institute and the Asia Pacific Exchange Foundation (formerly, the Far East Studies Institute). The staffers and members are exposed to a variety of sights and officials in China of particular interest to them. They are encouraged to ask questions and probe for insights about current conditions and policies in China. The resulting dialogue favors PRC government perspectives, but this is often offset by the American visitor's strong sense of the rapid economic growth and vibrant material life of China. On balance, it appears that such trips change attitudes of U.S. legislators in positive ways as far as China is concerned.

Another channel used by the Chinese government to influence U.S. decisionmaking is higher-level visits by Chinese officials. Two kinds are notable. The first is the occasional visit of Chinese officials charged with purchasing U.S. goods. Such "buying missions" garner considerable positive publicity, especially in regions where the purchases are made. In recent years, Beijing has sent such missions to make well-publicized purchases of U.S. grains, aircraft, and automobiles. A second type of high-level visit is that of senior leaders who represent Beijing's perspectives in important discussions with high-level U.S. administration and congressional leaders. When a senior Chinese official travels to Washington, meetings often are arranged not only with their U.S. counterparts but also with other officials concerned with the overall U.S.-China relationship. An example was the March 1996 visit of State Council official Liu Huaqiu. He met with his counterpart, National Security Advisor Anthony Lake, and held extensive talks with State Department, Defense Department, and congressional leaders, among others.[46]

The lobbying skills of Chinese embassy officials have improved somewhat in recent years, but from a very low base. In general, Beijing's efforts through this channel have been unsophisticated and ineffective.[47] Chinese officials have appeared more comfortable dealing with State Department and White House staff than with politicians on Capitol Hill. In the past, they have striven to build rapport with some senior-level officials who would presumably help to clarify PRC interests in administration deliberations on China-related questions. In Congress, they have followed a roughly similar approach, trying to work closely with offices that have cast votes and taken positions supportive of Chinese positions previously. In general, they have found it difficult to deal with adversaries and thus have lost opportunities to moderate the criticisms of the latter. Similarly, they often have not been active in working with those in Congress who are selective, eclectic, or wavering on an issue important to China.

The lobbying efforts of PRC officials are hampered by the Chinese government's insistence on casting so many issues in black-and-white terms. Beijing's "principled stand" on such issues as human rights and Taiwan are salient examples. As a result, Chinese officials have a tendency to tell U.S. officials what they expect the United States to do. They are less willing to compete in the realm of ideas and negotiated compromises or to recognize that a key to effective lobbying is learning over time.

In lobbying the U.S. government to delink MFN and human rights, it was probably just as well for PRC interests that the Chinese embassy adopted a low posture. Beijing had been successful in the previous two years in encouraging an unprecedented number of congressional members to visit China. Many staff delegations also visited at this time. Most returned with much greater appreciation of China's economic vibrancy and importance to the United States. More important, Beijing allowed U.S. business lobbyists to work unimpeded by possibly counterproductive actions from the Chinese embassy. Business lobbyists informed Chinese embassy staff of their general strategies and approaches, but Chinese officials decided that Beijing's interests would be better served by allowing U.S. business groups to speak for themselves, rather than to be seen as part of some coalition of forces led by the Chinese embassy officials.[48] Given the strongly negative U.S. media and public opinion about the Chinese government at the time, the low-key PRC embassy posture on lobbying over MFN was probably an appropriate one to achieve China's overall objective.

Notes

1. This section draws heavily and with permission from Jim Mann, "America and China's MFN Benefits: 1989-1994," draft paper distributed at American Assembly working group meeting, February 1995.

2. Ibid.

3. See, among others, Kenneth Lieberthal, *Governing China* (New York: Norton, 1995).

4. See analysis in *Congressional Quarterly Weekly Report*, late May-early June 1994. See also coverage in *New York Times, Washington Post, Washington Times*, for May 25 and May 26, 1994.

5. See analysis in *Congressional Quarterly Weekly Report*, late May-early June 1994. See also *New York Times, Washington Post, Washington Times*, for May 25 and 26, 1994.

6. Jim Mann, "America and China's MFN Benefits."

7. Ibid. See also Mann's review article in *Los Angeles Times,* September 11, 1996.

8. Jim Mann, "America and China's MFN Benefits."

9. Ibid. Discussions of American Assembly working group, February 1995 and December 1995.

10. For a review of congressional and related activities on this issue, see weekly coverage in *Congressional Quarterly Weekly Report.*

11. See *Congressional Quarterly Weekly Report.* See also Kerry Dumbaugh, *China-U.S. Relations*, CRS Issue Brief 94002.

12. It is important to remember the wide range of U.S. groups with an interest in China policy during this period. While the lobbying effort can be seen as a tug-of-war between groups led by business interests on one side, and human rights and labor groups on the other, a whole range of American organizations was actively considering policy options at this time. They ranged from various public affairs groups and scholarly and industrial organizations to religious groups with an interest in U.S. policy toward China. See the appendix for a listing of a sample of such organizations.

13. See Jim Mann, "America and China's MFN Benefits." See also Steven Teles, "Public Opinion and Interest Groups in the Making of U.S.-China Policy," conference paper, Harvard University, May 1996.

14. Reviewed in *China-U.S. Relations,* CRS Issue Brief 94002.

15. For an authoritative assessment of this issue, see David M. Lampton, "America's China Policy in the Age of the Finance Minister," *The China Quarterly* (1994): 597-621. This section also benefitted greatly from Steven Teles, "Public Opinion and Interest Groups in the Making of U.S.-China Policy"; Tricia Cortez, "Cash, Clash and Compromise," (thesis, Princeton University, April 3, 1996); and Steven Campbell, "Grass Roots vs. Coalition Lobbying: Transnational Strategies and the 1994 MFN Decision," (thesis, University of Louisville, December 1996).

16. See *Congressional Quarterly Weekly Report*, April 5, 1997.

17. See *Congressional Quarterly Weekly Report*, November 1, 1997, 2656-59.

18. See Steven Teles, "Public Opinion and Interest Groups in the Making of U.S.-China Policy." See also Steven Campbell, "Grass Roots Lobbying and Coalition Lobbying: Transnational Strategies and the 1994 MFN Decision."

19. This section draws heavily from Cortez, "Cash, Clash."

20. The U.S. business interest in the China market was no doubt related to a growing U.S. judgment that commercial law and the business climate in China were becoming sufficiently secure to allow for large-scale investments and other economic interactions.

21. Cited in Cortez, "Cash, Clash."

22. Ibid.

23. Peter H. Stone, "Big Business Favors China Trade," *Legal Times*, May 27, 1991.

24. Calman Cohen, chair of the Business Coalition for U.S.-China Trade and president of the Emergency Committee for American Trade (ECAT). Interview by Tricia N. Cortez, March 5, 1996, and cited in Cortez, "Cash, Clash."

25. Folsom, in ibid.

26. "Business Coalition Position Paper: Stabilizing and Improving U.S.-China Trade Relations," Business Coalition for U.S.-China Trade, February 1, 1996.

27. Cohen, in Cortez, "Cash, Clash."

28. This argument was the business community's key argument against human rights lobby groups and other MFN opponents, according to Peter Behr, "U.S. Business Waged Year-Long Lobbying Effort on China Trade," *Washington Post,* May 27, 1993.

29. Cited in Cortez, "Cash, Clash."

30. Joyce Barrett, "Shoe Retailers Lobby Senate on China MFN: China's MFN," *Footwear News* 47, no. 28 (July 15, 1991): 4.

31. T. R. Goldman, "Triple Teaming on MFN Status for China," *Legal Times,* May 30, 1994, and *ECAT Agenda 1996,* Emergency Committee for American Trade.

32. Cohen has lobbied Congress on trade issues for over ten years. In the past, he briefly served as Director of Congressional Affairs at the Office of the USTR during the Carter administration, and he also served on the professional staff of the U.S. Senate's Democratic Policy Committee.

33. Bruce Stokes, "Making a Mark on Trade Issues," *National Journal* (August 6, 1994).

34. China has sought to enter the WTO as a developing nation, which would grant it more trade privileges. Given China's economic growth, however, the U.S. business community generally wants China to enter as a developed nation.

35. Folsom, cited in Cortez, "Cash, Clash."

36. Taken from a U.S.-China Business Council membership packet.

37. Cited in Cortez, "Cash, Clash."

38. The council apparently does not engage in actual hands-on lobbying—that is left to members. Robert Kapp, "Relationship Building: U.S.-China Relations," *The China Business Review* 22, no. 5 (September 1995): 6.

39. *The China Business Review* (July 1995).

40. "U.S. Businesses in China to Lobby for MFN Renewal," *Reuters,* May 3, 1991.

41. *South China Morning Post,* August 15, 1993.

42. The eight trade associates are: the Recording Industry Association of America (RIAA); the National Music Publisher's Association (NMPA); the Association of American Publishers (AAP); the Business Software Alliance (BSA); the Interactive Digital Software Association (IDSA); the Information Technology Industry Council (ITI); the Motion Picture Association of America (MPAA); and the American Filmmakers Association (AFMA).

43. Cortez, "Cash, Clash," 67.

44. This seemed to have had an effect, as press coverage of Secretary Christopher's April 1994 visit to Beijing highlighted this line of argument made by U.S. business representatives in China.

45. Consultations, Washington, D.C., 1995-1996.

46. For details on high-level PRC visits to the United States, see the chronology that appears in each issue of *The China Quarterly.*

47. Consultations, Washington, D.C., 1995-1996.

48. Cortez, "Cash, Clash."

Chapter 5

The Taiwan Crisis of 1995-1996

The Taiwan crisis of 1995-1996 had deep roots in the respective policy aspirations and domestic politics of Taiwan, China, and the United States. Throughout most of the crisis, the United States was generally reactive in the face of competing pressures coming from Taiwan and the People's Republic of China. This Taiwan-PRC competition occurred in the context of the U.S. domestic debate over policy in Taiwan-PRC-United States triangular relations.[1]

During the previous two decades, the U.S.-PRC-Taiwan triangle, while often presenting problems, basically dovetailed with U.S. interests. The United States developed relations with the PRC while sustaining ties with Taiwan—all within an atmosphere promoting broad U.S. security and economic interests in Asian, Pacific, and world affairs. So the question naturally arose: where did the recent crisis come from? It was clearly not sought by the United States. Rather, the main catalyst was a changing Taiwan. As people on Taiwan have become economically advanced, better educated, more cosmopolitan, and politically democratic, they have demanded that their leaders adopt a policy to end Taiwan's status as an international pariah. Taiwan leaders who run against this tide fare poorly in elections.

In response to changing domestic circumstances, Taiwan's leaders are prepared to use Taiwan's influence as one of the world's largest trading nations and holder of one of the world's largest reserves of foreign currency to achieve greater international recognition and respect. Using financial resources to attract international attention, Taiwan develops economic and political relationships with important countries and seeks broader political influence and respect for the people of Taiwan and their democratically elected leaders.[2]

Taiwan's growing assertiveness ran up against PRC assertiveness. After the 1989 Tiananmen incident and the collapse of communism in the Soviet bloc, Chinese leaders were beleaguered and fairly isolated in world politics. But taking advantage of the international attention its remarkable economic growth has garnered, China reversed its situation through effective economic policies and adroit diplomacy. All major powers, with the possible exception of the United States, have acknowledged the legitimacy of China's leaders and have developed close ties to capitalize on economic and other opportunities.

This diplomatic success fueled Chinese international activism. Beijing has pressed its claim to disputed territories in the South China Sea. It drove a hard bargain with world powers striving to achieve a comprehensive nuclear test ban. It continued missile and nuclear-related technology transfers to Pakistan and Iran that have been opposed by the United States. It also is prepared to go head-to-head with the United States in threatening sanctions and countersanctions over economic disputes ranging from most-favored-nation tariff treatment to market access and intellectual property rights.

Just as Taiwan's foreign policy has been pushed by domestic pressures and politics, it appears that domestic influences have contributed to PRC assertiveness.[3] Chinese leaders have fostered an atmosphere of nationalism that portrays China, rightly, as a past victim of international pressures. It implies that China now has the moral high ground in reasserting its claim to disputed territories and world leadership that were lost during the age of imperialism. As a result, it is difficult for Chinese leaders to propose policies suggesting that Beijing should compromise its claims to Taiwan or disputed territories and its terms for membership in international bodies such as the WTO. Moreover, the leadership succession in the PRC, as Deng Xiaoping slowly faded and ultimately died in February 1997, seem to reinforce the PRC's stance. During the transition, it appeared to be difficult for leaders to promote policy that suggested compromise of China's moral right to its nationalistic aspirations. Conciliatory policies could be used against them in the ongoing struggle for power.

Taiwan and the PRC have long competed for influence in the United States. Yet for some time in the latter 1980s and early 1990s, the competition was not as acute as it has been more recently. Although PRC leaders were concerned over democratization in Taiwan and the attendant rise of pro-independence politicians, they were also encouraged by how democratization in Taiwan was forcing Taipei leaders to open economic and other contacts with the mainland. In short, Beijing endeavored to use growing cross-strait economic, social, and cultural contacts to build ties with Taiwan that would offset the perceived negative trend caused by Taiwan's growing assertiveness for international recognition. Meanwhile, U.S. policymakers made clear to both the PRC and Taiwan the broad outlines of U.S.-China policy. Both Taiwan and Beijing had come to terms with this consensus in U.S.-China policy in the latter 1980s.

The context of policymaking changed after the Tiananmen incident and the end of the cold war. The Bush administration was able to protect the broad guidelines of policy toward the PRC and Taiwan despite heavy pressure from the media, Congress, and interest groups. However, the Clinton administration was not as strongly fixed. As noted earlier, it entered office on a platform decidedly critical of China and soon changed Bush administration policy by linking China's MFN trade status to its human rights practices, only to end linkage in the face of heavy pressure from the PRC, U.S. businesses with an interest in China, and opinion leaders. The lesson both for Taiwan and the PRC in their newly assertive approaches and for organized groups in the United States seemed clear: the Clinton administration did not possess a strongly fixed policy, and pressures could be applied in the hope of prompting policy change favoring one side or the other.

The Lee Teng-hui Visit and U.S.-PRC-Taiwan Relations

The Clinton administration's decision, responding to congressional pressure, to allow Taiwan President Lee Teng-hui's Cornell University visit in June 1995 prompted an extraordinary reaction by the PRC. Beijing issued strong protests, held up or canceled important bilateral dialogues, suspended key meetings with Taiwan, and conducted provocative military exercises near Taiwan. It warned that a Taiwan move toward de jure independence would lead to a PRC invasion of Taiwan and a protracted cold war with the United States.[4]

The decision to allow Lee Teng-hui to visit the United States not only resulted in the suspension of diplomatic and other official ties, but even more important it fostered within China a strongly negative view of U.S. policy intentions.[5] This reinforced prior PRC suspicions that the United States had decided to "contain" China. For some time, Chinese government officials and military officers held that the United States opposed the rise of China and adopted corresponding policies, including improved relations with Taiwan, to "hold back" China. Despite the lively debate and widely divergent opinions in the United States over many issues in U.S.-China relations, Chinese leaders have maintained that U.S. policymakers think and act in coordination, focusing on China's growing power as a threat to the United States and stressing that the United States must weaken China through security, economic, and political measures.

The Clinton administration tried to reassure Beijing that the United

States was not attempting to contain China's development, but Chinese officials remained unmoved. In June and July 1995, Beijing indicated that only "concrete" action by the U.S. government—at minimum a pledge by the Clinton administration that it would not give a visa to other senior Taiwan leaders—would allow U.S.-China relations to go forward. To underline the point, Beijing called home its ambassador, refused the U.S. offer to send Undersecretary of State Peter Tarnoff to China for talks, and rebuffed reported U.S. queries about a possible U.S.-China summit. Beijing also escalated political and military pressure on Taiwan and Lee Teng-hui in particular.[6]

The thaw began on August 1, 1995, when Secretary of State Christopher and Chinese Foreign Minister Qian Qichen met in Brunei.[7] Christopher confirmed that the United States would not promise to prohibit senior Taiwan visitors from traveling in a private capacity to the United States. However, some Chinese officials pointed to U.S. reassurances, including a letter from President Clinton to Chinese leaders, reaffirming past U.S. policy on Taiwan. Soon after the meeting in Brunei, China altered its view of U.S. policy. PRC officials acknowledged that Washington was not working to contain China; nonetheless, they privately said that unnamed senior leaders in Beijing continued to believe this.[8] Chinese leaders also endorsed interaction with Congress. Foreign Minister Qian stated on August 18 that "China is willing to increase contacts and exchanges with the U.S. Congress and welcomes more U.S. congressmen to visit China."[9] Beijing also reversed policy by agreeing to a visit by Undersecretary Tarnoff and by discussing plans for a U.S.-China summit. For the first time it expressed willingness to accept former-Sen. James Sasser as ambassador to China[10] and returned its ambassador to Washington. China also improved the overall atmosphere in U.S.-China relations by releasing the detained human rights activist Harry Wu after his conviction in August, easing the way for Hillary Clinton to attend the International Women's Conference in Beijing in September.

The October 24, 1995, meeting in New York between Presidents Clinton and Jiang Zemin proceeded smoothly despite wrangling over the protocol level and the site of the meeting.[11] U.S. and Chinese officials portrayed the session at New York's Lincoln Center as the most positive of the three sessions held by the two leaders since 1993.[12] China's moderate approach to the United States stood in marked contrast to Beijing's continued harsh pressure against Lee Teng-hui. In effect, Chinese officials and media now acknowledged that Lee's visit reflected more the strong desire of Lee and others in Taiwan to assume a greater role in international affairs than it did a U.S. conspiracy to use the "Taiwan card" to check the growth of Chinese power and influence.

Lessons Learned—The PRC

Chinese officials and specialists consulted in the latter part of 1995 gleaned several lessons from the crisis over Taiwan.[13] Many in China recognized that Beijing overplayed its hand in pressing the United States for "concrete" pledges against Taiwan official visits and in pushing the Taiwan people to abandon Lee Teng-hui in favor of a leader more committed to reunification. Beijing also appeared to recognize that charges of U.S. "containment" and avoidance of dialogue until the United States proved otherwise strengthened the hands of those suspicious of China and weakened the arguments of administration officials and members of Congress who argued for moderate approaches.

Interest in a working relationship with the United States encouraged China to develop common ground in U.S.-China relations and to play down bilateral differences. Beijing tried to use Jiang's October 24, 1995, meeting with Clinton in New York for this purpose. After the meeting, Chinese officials privately made known China's interest in a "smooth" relationship with the Clinton administration. Whereas in mid-1995 Beijing simply awaited the results of the 1996 presidential election, some Chinese officials now averred that working constructively with the current administration was in China's best interest. In particular, they said Beijing now understood that domestic pressure from a wide array of critics of China in Congress and the media and the debate over China policy in the 1996 presidential campaign could destabilize relations. Beijing thus decided to try to develop closer relations with the administration.

China also was determined to do a better job of influencing U.S. politics. Jiang Zemin told U.S. reporters in mid-October 1995 that lobbying Congress would be an important priority in the year ahead. As is discussed following, it was around this time that the Chinese government began to strengthen its embassy's congressional relations staff and established a formal working group under the PRC state council's senior foreign policy expert, Liu Huaqiu, to deal with Congress. Meanwhile, later press reports and congressional investigation also focused on this period as the time when PRC leaders allegedly began using money in both legal and illegal ways to influence U.S. election politics.

China's U.S. specialists also said that the PRC would put more effort into winning support from other U.S. sectors, notably the media and business.[14] Chinese officials also acknowledged that Beijing's invective against Lee Teng-hui had strengthened support for Lee on Taiwan. Ultimately, China would need to adjust its hard line to open a dialogue with Taiwan.

Many Chinese officials nonetheless continued to emphasize the delicate condition of U.S.-China relations. Some Chinese leaders remained suspicious of U.S. intentions toward China. Others, more flexible and moderate, had little confidence that the United States would develop policy on sensitive issues like Taiwan that would avoid a future crisis. In their view, the United States lacked a clear sense of priorities toward China in particular and foreign policy in general. As a result, Washington dealt with issues on a case-by-case basis, making it difficult to predict U.S. policy. The Clinton administration's reversal on the Lee Teng-hui visit was said to represent just such a phenomenon. Chinese specialists feared that without a sense of order and priorities in U.S. policy toward China, similar policy reversals could occur with clearly negative results for U.S.-China relations.

Lessons Learned—The U.S. Congress[15]

Clinton administration officials and many in Congress acknowledged that Beijing's harsh response to the Lee Teng-hui visit took them by surprise and that the United States needed to exercise greater care in dealing with Taiwan-related issues. Because the Lee visit reflected congressional pressure on the administration, the effect of PRC actions on congressional attitudes was most important in determining U.S. policy.

Some congressional officials acknowledged that in the aftermath of the PRC's 1995 military maneuvers directed at Taiwan, Congress had pulled back on Taiwan-related issues. In part, this reflected greater discretion by Taiwan, which adopted a lower profile on Capitol Hill in the second half of 1995. It also reflected the wish of many members to avoid difficulties in the U.S.-PRC-Taiwan triangular relationship. Thus, H.R. 63—expressing support for Taiwan's representation in the UN—was delayed because some members of Congress believed that raising and passing the resolution would undermine U.S. interests with China and Taiwan. Such resolutions passed in previous sessions of Congress.

On the other hand, some members of Congress not normally associated with a hard-line policy became more rigid after Beijing's mid-1995 military exercises. They suspected that Beijing used military force not only to cow Taiwan but also to intimidate the United States and test the will of an administration seen by some as irresolute in foreign policy. This bipartisan group wanted the United States to stand firm on Taiwan and related issues and urged the president not to "reward" PRC "temper tantrums." They also believed that the United States was within its rights under agreements with the PRC to allow Lee Teng-hui to visit Cornell University in a private capacity. Some members asserted that the administration did not respond strongly enough to the PRC military exercises in the Taiwan Strait, which included missile test firings in July 1995.

Renewed Crisis—March 1996

The thaw in U.S.-China relations in late 1995 was only temporary. Despite the avowed interest of some Chinese officials in maintaining smooth U.S.-China relations during the election year, renewed military pressure on Taiwan and other rigid PRC policies on economic, proliferation, and human rights issues prompted a sharply negative reaction in the United States. Press reports in late January 1996 that Chinese officials were accompanying military intimidation tactics toward Taiwan with threats to attack U.S. cities in the event U.S. forces intervened in the Taiwan Strait stiffened media and congressional attitudes.[16]

China's provocative use of force in the Taiwan Strait in March 1996, timed to coincide with Taiwan's first presidential election, headed the list of U.S. grievances. Other major issues included the estimated $2 billion in losses U.S. firms suffered annually as a result of China's violations of U.S. intellectual property rights, despite past Chinese agreement to halt such violations; China's reported continued cooperation with Pakistan's effort to build a nuclear-weapons capability; reports of China's sale of surface-to-surface missiles and related technology to Iran and Pakistan;[17] and Beijing's hard-line stance toward any signs of political dissent.[18]

In the face of a deluge of media criticism and congressional and interest group pressures on the Clinton administration's comprehensive engagement policy, the White House toughened its stance. During PRC military exercises near Taiwan in March 1996, it deployed two U.S. carrier battle groups in the area, postponed the visit of China's defense minister to the United States, and suspended approval of Export-Import Bank financing for new projects in China pending a review of options to deal with reported Chinese export of nuclear-related technologies. However, the administration also tried to sustain long-term engagement through dialogue between U.S. and PRC senior leaders. President Clinton reportedly gave newly appointed U.S. Ambassador James Sasser a letter for China's leaders requesting such a dialogue. China responded by sending to Washington in March 1996 Liu Huaqiu, the State Council's senior foreign policy expert, for discussions with White House and congressional leaders.[19]

Far from assuaged by the administration's actions, Congress sought additional measures to reinforce the U.S. posture. The House and Senate passed separate nonbinding resolutions expressing support for Taiwan in the face of PRC intimidation. Many members were adamant that the administration should adopt a stronger response to reported Chinese nuclear and missile proliferation and to violations of the intellectual property rights of U.S. businesses. The House and the Senate also passed the 1996-1997 State Department authorization bill (H.R. 1561), which contained over a dozen provisions targeted directly or indirectly at strengthening U.S. policy on Taiwan, Tibet, human rights, and Chinese membership in the World Trade Organization.[20] President Clinton vetoed the bill and a veto override failed in the House.

Following Lee Teng-hui's election, a strong showing that gathered 54 percent of the vote in a field of four candidates, both Taipei and Beijing took steps to ease bilateral tensions. However, the U.S. show of naval power in the face of PRC military exercises brought the situation in the strait and in U.S.-PRC relations to a new and important juncture. In particular, after several months when Washington and Beijing had managed to ease their earlier tension over Taiwan, the United States was once again of central and immediate importance in PRC policy toward Taiwan.

Competing Groups on Taiwan Policy: Status and Outlook

After the crisis of 1996, the Clinton administration tried to deal more effectively with the tug-of-war for influence that has characterized U.S. policy on the U.S.-Taiwan-PRC triangular relationship in recent years. But much depended on the inclination of pro-Taiwan and pro-PRC forces in the United States.[21]

In particular, for the reasons noted earlier, PRC-Taiwan competition for international recognition and other rewards is likely to continue and perhaps intensify. Both Taipei and Beijing have strong domestic political and other reasons to continue an assertive approach in world politics. Further, for Taiwan, the search for international space appears to be part of a strategy designed to secure Taiwan's separate status at a time of growing PRC economic and military power. For their part, PRC leaders recognize that China needs to control Taiwan if it expects to play a truly great power role in Asian and world affairs. A China preoccupied with an unfriendly or uncooperative Taiwan along its seaward periphery promises to be a much weaker influence in international politics than a reunified China, according to this view.

As in the past, the main international arena for this competition will be Washington. If recent past practice is any guide, the outcome of U.S. policy may be an incremental drift, moving in one direction or another depending on the relative strength of arguments and domestic forces pushing U.S. policy in one direction or the other. Thus, it seems useful to consider an inventory of the organized groups and other domestic forces in the United States with an interest in these issues and their respective arguments.

On one side are leaders in the Clinton administration and others who argue that China is very important. The U.S. relationship with China is clearly at a delicate stage. U.S. policy needs to move relations with China back on track. In this way the United States can better foster tendencies toward economic, social, and political change advantageous to the United States and encourage greater Chinese interdependence in world affairs.

As far as Taiwan is concerned, some of these officials privately aver that Taiwan is dependent on the United States. There is no need for the United States to assuage feelings in Taiwan with actions sure to antagonize the PRC. Taiwan will basically have to do what the United States wants, their argument goes. Thus the United States should play down its relations with Taiwan so it can build ties with the PRC.

Opposed to this view are many in Congress, the media, and elsewhere who emphasize Taiwan's positive features for the United States. Politically, economically, and in other ways, closer U.S. relations with Taiwan give particular and often concrete benefits to a wide range of Americans. Taiwan has long-term strategic value worthy of preserving. Other advantages include trade and investment opportunities, campaign contributions, and votes of Taiwanese-American blocs. Consonant with American ideology and values, Taiwan's free-market enterprise and recent democratization have attracted much support. In contrast, many U.S. observers are skeptical of any significant movement of the PRC toward political pluralism or international interdependence. Finally, there is a continued asymmetry of power between the United States and China. China will press the United States on Taiwan or other questions only when it senses weakness. If the United States is strong and demonstrates negative consequences for Beijing if it follows a confrontational approach, PRC leaders will pull back, the argument goes. They will do so because of a perceived need to continue workable relations with a world power.

Which side will win this debate on U.S. policy? Past experience since President Nixon's opening to the PRC over twenty years ago shows that on big decisions, the PRC won and Taiwan lost. The pattern is clear in Nixon's initial visit to China; the decline in U.S. support for Taiwan's seat at the U.N.; the U.S. decision to normalize diplomatic relations with Beijing; and the U.S. decision to sign the 1982 communiqué limiting U.S. arms sales to Taiwan. Yet for the most part, those decisions were heavily influenced by an overriding strategic rationale that drove U.S. policy toward the PRC and against the Soviet Union.

Even when the PRC was winning the big U.S. decisions, Taiwan was making important incremental gains. In the period since the 1978 U.S. decision to break official ties with Taiwan for the sake of relations with the PRC, Americans have—with the support of Taiwan and U.S. groups backing Taiwan—increased the breadth and scope of relations in several important ways. This was seen notably in various provisions added to the initial draft of the Taiwan Relations Act; backing for Taiwan's standing in the Asian Development Bank; support for Taiwan's development of a new, indigenous fighter aircraft; endorsing Taiwan's membership in GATT; increasingly high-level interchange between U.S. and Taiwan leaders; facilitating Taiwan's entry into APEC; President Bush's decision to sell 150 F-16 fighters to Taiwan; and the 1995 decision on Lee Teng-hui's trip to Cornell.[22]

The end of the cold war terminated the strategic rationale underlying the pro-PRC decisions in U.S. policy in the 1970s and 1980s. As noted following, a new strategy has begun to emerge—i.e., China has great and growing power and therefore is very important in its own right. Today, however, this view does not automatically mean that U.S. policy will tilt irrevocably toward the PRC. There is, of course, the view that because China is becoming so strong and important, and is pressing the United States hard on the Taiwan issue and other questions, the United States should endeavor to accommodate China over Taiwan. Nonetheless, an alternative to this approach has arisen, particularly as Beijing has used its new strength to attempt to intimidate Taiwan, the United States, and regional powers. Further, if China and the United States eventually become strategic opponents, Taiwan would be advantageously situated, an asset for either. Thus, China's importance, strength, and assertiveness in this line of argument have the effect of strengthening U.S. resolve to support Taiwan against Beijing's threat.

It seems that this inventory of U.S. domestic forces and their arguments on the Taiwan issue show that whatever administration is voted in, it will face strong pressure from people in the media, Congress, and elsewhere who feel the United States should do more to help Taiwan. The main counterargument will be that such a course risks trouble with an increasingly powerful China. This counterargument cuts two ways, however: one way toward U.S. accommodation of the PRC over Taiwan; the other way toward increasing U.S. firmness toward the PRC. The result may be a U.S. policy that in general sides with Taiwan. This will be contingent—among other things—on Taiwan's continuing a close and cooperative relationship with the United States and avoiding provocative actions that could be interpreted as seriously exacerbating cross-strait relations.

Looking to the near future, it appears that Taiwan would want to avoid strong efforts to press for change in U.S. policy on at least three grounds. First, as noted following, the U.S. administration, with some congressional support, has undertaken a new approach to China focused increasingly on high-level meetings leading to U.S.-PRC summits in 1997 and 1998. Taiwan presumably would not wish to appear as trying deliberately to "spoil" the atmosphere for such exchanges deemed important by key U.S. leaders. Second, press disclosures beginning in October and November 1996 focused on alleged Taiwan efforts to seek special treatment from U.S. officials by using possibly illegal political campaign contributions. Against this backdrop, pro-Taiwan forces in the United States would presumably be reluctant to launch special efforts to gain greater attention from the U.S. government. Third, while maintaining steady pressure against Taiwan's efforts to seek greater international recognition, Beijing leaders do not appear prepared for the time being to launch major new military attacks or other moves to intimidate Taiwan. They appear preoccupied by the complicated reversion of Hong Kong to PRC control, the leadup to and follow-through from China's 15th Communist Party Congress, and the U.S.-China summits.

The Tug-of-War over Taiwan: Influential Organized Interests

The lopsided congressional votes in 1995 favoring Lee Teng-hui's visit demonstrated that pro-Taiwan sentiment was strong and rising in the United States. U.S. observers opposing confrontation with the PRC on this question were limited to relatively small groups within the administration, especially the State Department and some White House staff. Once Beijing reacted as strongly as it did to Lee's visit, pro-Taiwan organized groups were put on the defensive in the face of a variety of U.S. interests—business, strategic, and political, among others. These interests did not want to jeopardize U.S.-China relations on account of U.S. gestures toward Taiwan. The most effective proponents were the business groups noted earlier in the section dealing with MFN for China.

Interests on the Taiwan side of the debate were led by the Taiwan government and related interests in Taiwan and by their extensive lobbying and other networks of influence in the United States.[23] The multifaceted Taiwan effort saw hiring of lobbyists; grants to U.S. institutions, think tanks, universities, and individual researchers for work of interest to Taiwan; and extensive public relations efforts by the Taiwan government and the government's offices in the United States, especially the Taipei Economic and Cultural Representative Office (TECRO)—a de facto embassy in Washington, D.C., backed by over a dozen de facto consulates around the country.

The basic strategy of this pro-Taiwan effort in recent years has been to seek incremental improvement in the treatment of Taiwan by the U.S. government. It does so first by building goodwill among a wide range of key U.S. opinion leaders and decisionmakers. This involves interaction with such groups as editorial writers and reporters, local and national legislative and executive officials, scholars and policy analysts, and business groups. TECRO officials and others build long-lasting relationships with these Americans, who often are invited for expense-paid trips to Taiwan. Taiwan officials also facilitate purchases of U.S.-produced goods and investment in U.S. locales. Indeed, the PRC government's recent efforts to send so-called purchasing missions to buy products in the United States, and to encourage congressional members and staff to visit China, are modeled on efforts pioneered by Taiwan. In general, Americans affected by these efforts are impressed by the dynamism and economic prosperity of Taiwan and appreciative of the material benefits that come to them or their institutions or localities as a result of grants, trade, investment, or other exchanges.

In recent years, Taiwan officials, lobbyists, and others have found it easier to build goodwill among broad segments of American society. On the one hand, American observers warmly welcome Taiwan's record in economic development and political democratization. Taiwan research and travel grants ensure that U.S. scholars, reporters, editorial writers, policy analysts, and others are made fully aware of recent Taiwan developments. These are supplemented by numerous conferences, study-group efforts, and other research-analysis activities in the United States that are supported by money and personnel sent from Taiwan.

On the other hand is the decidedly more negative American experience and attitude toward the communist, authoritarian PRC government. This makes U.S. observers less accommodating to PRC demands over Taiwan and other issues. It also makes Taiwan's recent moves toward democracy stand out in even sharper, positive contrast.

For many years after the break in U.S.-Taiwan diplomatic relations, Taiwan officials placed their emphasis on developing an ever broadening and deepening U.S. support for Taiwan to improve the substance of U.S. relations with Taiwan. This involved seeking incremental improvements, such as greater access to high-level U.S. officials, more sophisticated U.S. arms for sale to Taiwan, and greater U.S. support for Taiwan's representation in such international organizations as the Asian Development Bank, APEC, and GATT. The approach was designed to avoid, if possible, a major confrontation with the PRC, but at the same time advancing Taiwan's interests politically, economically, and militarily. Some Taiwan officials feared that if a major crisis were to arise, the United States would be forced to choose between Beijing and Taipei. They realized that since the 1970s, the United States had sided with Beijing on such big decisions as normalization of relations or curbing arms sales to Taiwan. As a result, they thought that a lower-key approach seeking incremental gains was in Taiwan's best interest.

The methods used by the Taiwan government to build goodwill have involved a great increase in TECRO lobbying personnel. Now having thirteen regional offices in the United States, TECRO works painstakingly to build grassroots support. Its representatives are increasingly sophisticated, knowledgeable, and able to command greater resources. Each TECRO office is staffed with career diplomats, information specialists, trade representatives, and cultural officials headed by senior supervisors handling public relations as well as network-building tasks.

In the lobbying effort leading to Lee Teng-hui's visit in 1995, the Taiwan government, mainly through TECRO, invited leading U.S. media reporters and representatives to Taiwan. Prominent U.S. think-tank and other opinion leaders also were invited. The trips were capped by an hour-long meeting with Lee Teng-hui. Meanwhile, an unprecedented stream of Taiwan officials traveled to Washington, making their case for better treatment by the United States. Additional lobbyists were hired to encourage U.S. decisionmakers to support Lee's visit, to allow Taiwan to join the UN, and to support other measures designed to win greater international recognition.

As noted earlier, the more intense Taiwan lobbying prior to the Lee Teng-Hui visit was motivated in part by Taiwan domestic politics. Lee's ruling Nationalist Party needed to show that its approach to foreign affairs was having some concrete success in order to counter the charges of the opposition Democratic Progressive Party (DPP). The DPP charged that Taiwan remained diplomatically isolated because it refused to break from the one-China stance of the past and allow the Taiwan people to determine their future status through a plebescite. Lee and the Nationalists judged that such a vote might lead to results that would prompt the PRC to attack Taiwan.

Since the early 1980s, many Taiwanese-American interest groups have coalesced in an organization, the Formosan Association for Public Affairs (FAPA), that has encouraged a U.S. policy more supportive of Taiwan's autonomy and self-determination. In general, FAPA's policy positions have been in line with those in the DPP, stressing Taiwan's right to self-determination; they have been sharply critical of the ruling Nationalists' continued adherence to a one-China stance. Pressure on Lee and the Nationalists' position in the United States increased in 1995 when the DPP established its own representative office in Washington, D.C. Led by Parris Chang, a prominent China specialist in U.S. academic circles who had returned to Taiwan to enter the legislature in 1993, the office pursued lobbying efforts supporting Lee's visit to the United States and encouraging further U.S. steps to back Taiwan's autonomy and right of self-determination.

The strong PRC military reaction to Lee's visit vividly demonstrated the dangers of the DPP approach and also prompted Lee Teng-hui's Nationalists to revert to the more low-key, incremental approach of the past. Nonetheless, Taiwan officials and other representatives lost few opportunities to build on American goodwill as well as the strong positive media image Taiwan conveyed as it held its democratic election and gave majority support to Lee Teng-hui despite Beijing's military threats and intimidation. In the weeks after the elections, for example, most major universities and think tanks in the Washington, D.C., area and many others elsewhere held conferences and related public events on the elections and the crisis in the Taiwan Strait. These meetings had a number of features in common:

- Taiwan interest groups had good relations with the sponsoring U.S. organizations because of past contacts, usually involving Taiwan financial and other support.
- Taiwan interest groups bore a substantial share of the expenses for the conferences and related public events on the elections and the cross-strait crisis.
- Prominent English-speaking scholar-officials from Taiwan were featured at the meetings.
- The conferences and related events attracted a wide range of media, political, and governmental leaders in addition to scholars and policy experts.
- The meetings often included the point of view of PRC scholars or scholar-officials. These scholars adhere mostly to Beijing's hard line on Taiwan. As a result, the U.S. media, political, government, and other participants tended to show more sympathy for the interests of a democratizing and "progressive" Taiwan, in the face of a "repressive" and "domineering" Beijing.
- While receiving organizational and funding support through TECRO and other Taiwan government and nongovernment sources, the meetings sometimes also had the support of Taiwanese-American groups and the DPP office in the United States.[24]

Notes

1. This is based heavily on a conference paper of the same title the author presented at conferences at Harvard University and Beijing University in mid-1996 and on the discussion at those conferences. See also CRS Issue Brief 96032 and other publications cited in the additional reading section of that brief.

2. Press reports in October and November 1996 highlighted the alleged large contributions to U.S. political campaigns made by Taiwan government and other interests. See the *Wall Street Journal,* November 1, 1996, and *New York Times*, November 1, 1996.

3. See, among others, Shambaugh, "Exploring the Complexities of Contemporary Taiwan," *The China Quarterly* 148 (December 1996): 1045-54.

4. For background, see Robert Sutter, *China's Sinister View of U.S. Policy,* CRS Report 95-750S, June 26, 1995.

5. For details on China's cutting of ties with the United States and other reactions to the Taiwan president's visit, see Robert Sutter, *China Policy. Managing U.S.-PRC-Taiwan Relations after President Lee's Visit to the U.S.,* CRS Report 95-727S, June 19, 1995.

6. For background see *China-U.S. Relations*, CRS Issue Brief 94002, and *Taiwan*, CRS Issue Brief 96032.

7. *Los Angeles Times,* August 2, 1995.

8. Consultations, Washington, D.C., and New York, August 23, 25, and 26, 1995.

9. New China News Agency, August 18, 1995.

10. Radio Beijing, August 2, 1995.

11. For background, see *China-U.S. Relations,* CRS Issue Brief 94002.

12. *New York Times,* October 25, 1995.

13. Consultations, Washington, D.C., and New York, August 23, 25 and 26, 1995. Also, consultations, Beijing, December 16-20, 1995.

14. *U.S. News and World Report* (October 23, 1995): 72.

15. See Robert Sutter, *China Policy—Crisis Over Taiwan 1995*, CRS Report 95-1173F, December 5, 1995.

16. *New York Times*, January 24, 1996.

17. See Shirley Kan, *Chinese Proliferation of Weapons of Mass Destruction: Background and Analysis,* CRS Report 96-767F, September 13, 1996.

18. For background see Kerry Dumbaugh, *China-U.S. Relations,* CRS Issue Brief 94002.

19. Reviewed in Robert Sutter and Dianne Rennack, *China, Congress and Sanctions,* CRS Report 96-348F, April 17, 1996, 1-2.

20. Ibid., 1-2.

21. The framework for this analysis is taken notably from a detailed discussion of this issue at a Heritage Foundation seminar, Washington, D.C., March 5, 1996.

22. For discussion of these steps, see, among others, *Taiwan—U.S. Policy Choices,* CRS Issue Brief 96032.

23. For an authoritative overview of the impact of pro-Taiwan lobbying on U.S. policy, see I Yuan, "Tyranny of the Status Quo: The Taiwan Lobby's Impact on U.S.-Taiwan Relations," conference paper, George Washington University, June 17, 1995. See also relevant discussion in Nancy B. Tucker, *Taiwan, Hong Kong and the U.S.* (New York: Twayne, 1994), and Thomas Robinson, "America in Taiwan's Post-Cold War Foreign Relations," *The China Quarterly* 148 (December 1996): 1340-61. See also widespread press coverage in *Wall Street Journal, New York Times, Los Angeles Times, Washington Times,* and *Washington Post* in October and November 1996 dealing with pro-Taiwan lobbying in the United States.

24. For background, see Thomas Robinson, "America in Taiwan's Post-Cold War Foreign Relations," *The China Quarterly* 148 (December 1996): 1340-61. For specific information see CRS Memorandum to Congressional China Watchers dated May 13, 1996.

Chapter 6

Convergence and Conflict in U.S.-China Policy, 1996-1997

The crisis in U.S.-China relations over Taiwan in 1995 and 1996 prompted the Clinton administration to pay more attention to China policy. As time wore on, it became apparent that senior U.S. administration officials, and some in Congress, were moving toward a clearer and more consistent set of priorities and actions in dealing with China. This opened the way for higher-level meetings and U.S.-PRC summits. At the same time, however, the forward movement in U.S. policy mobilized those who remained opposed to China for various reasons. The controversy over alleged pro-China forces giving U.S. candidates illegal campaign contributions for a time weakened the administration's position and strengthened the critics.[1]

With strong urging from Congress, President Clinton took a tough public stance in 1996 toward Beijing's use of force near Taiwan and systematic PRC violations of U.S. intellectual property rights. Along a different track, the Clinton administration tried to find common ground with China through high-level communications and face-to-face meetings.

It became clear that administration messages and negotiations with senior Chinese leaders in 1996 were part of a broader trend, albeit still tentative, in U.S. policy toward China. Long pulled in different directions by various competing interests and concerns, U.S. policy toward China was coming together in less conflicted patterns. Evidence included:

- President Clinton's more carefully calibrated use of positive and negative incentives in dealing with China issues in 1996. The show of force in the Taiwan Strait and the president's tough posture on intellectual property rights balanced the administration's renewal of most-favored-nation (MFN) tariff treatment for China and its reaching an understanding with Beijing concerning a sale of nuclear-related equipment to Pakistan.

- Sen. Bob Dole's policy speech on Asia on May 9, 1996, which avoided wide difference with the overall direction of Clinton administration China policy, though he castigated the administration's "inept" handling of the U.S.-China relationship in the past three years.
- Repeated Clinton administration private messages and public speeches regarding the U.S. desire for a more constructive relationship, leading to National Security Adviser Lake's visit to China in early summer 1996, which paved the way for U.S.-China summit meetings and other high-level contacts. President Clinton and Chinese President Jiang Zemin confirmed that there would be high-level meetings, including summit meetings in 1997 and 1998, during their meeting at the Asian Pacific Economic Cooperation (APEC) summit in the Philippines in November 1996.
- Generally low-key efforts by U.S. critics to cut off MFN tariff treatment for China during the annual debate in Congress in 1996.
- Important congressional leaders' assertions that "punishing" China through withdrawal of MFN privileges or other means needed to be replaced by a more carefully crafted and less mutually injurious effort by the United States to "deal" with China's rise.

The Rise of China

The Clinton administration, some officials in Congress, and other U.S. elites became cognizant of China's rising wealth and power and the many challenges this poses for U.S. policy. They increasingly saw China as a very large, strategically located country undergoing rapid economic growth and social change yet ruled by authoritarian political leaders. A combination of rising Chinese power and nationalistic assertiveness poses serious problems for the United States in many realms: security interests in Asia; efforts to curb trafficking in technology for weapons of mass destruction; support for a smooth-running, market-based international economic system; and backing of other international norms regarding human rights, environmental protection, and other issues.[2]

Historical experience suggests that the United States will not reach any "grand bargain" or lasting solution to the China challenge. Many U.S. leaders have perceived that they will need to devote continuous high-level policy attention, issue by issue, case by case, year by year, in order to deter excessive Chinese assertiveness and to encourage Chinese accommodation to prevailing international practice. In so doing, the United States would be ill-served to rely solely on policies designed to moderate Chinese assertiveness through accommodation and greater integration in world affairs. Although many are hopeful about the positive changes that could come from China's economic modernization and social change, they could be long in coming.

As a result, U.S. policymakers have tried to establish U.S. goals vis-à-vis China and to clearly define negative and positive incentives that would prompt PRC behavior more compatible with U.S. interests. The show of force off Taiwan and the threat of U.S. trade sanctions represented clear negative incentives, while the promise of summit meetings represented a positive incentive. At the same time, a U.S. policy of containment against China has been seen as both premature and, in current circumstances, largely unworkable.

Effective U.S. strategy toward China is arguably best pursued within a broader U.S. strategy in Asia—one including a strong military, economic, and political presence, requiring some degree of cooperation from important U.S. allies and friends in the region.

Recent administration-led efforts to establish a more consistent, attentive, high-level U.S. relationship with China have overcome some obstacles at home and abroad. In the United States, public opinion has remained decidedly negative toward China, and the U.S. media have continued the practice of highlighting Chinese practices and policies that affront American interests and values. Those American interest groups sharply critical of Beijing have remained active, despite their weak showing in the annual congressional debate in 1996 on MFN for China.

In China, senior leaders have voiced approval of Clinton administration initiatives and have modified the negative PRC media line in opposition to an alleged U.S. "containment" policy directed at China. Nevertheless, PRC officials and public opinion remain wary and suspicious of U.S. intentions. Some in China suspect that U.S. officials are opportunistic in making dramatic charges for tactical advantage. Chinese suspicions are reinforced by a strong sense of nationalism and uncertain leadership politics in China.

At the least, the improvement helped to stabilize relations after the crisis over Taiwan and minimized U.S.-China policy issues during the 1996 presidential election campaign; it appeared to affect Chinese politics comparably during the run-up to the 1997 party congress. More optimistic assessments say that the U.S. administration is serious about moving senior-level interchange with China forward on a wide range of issues, and China is ready to respond in order to advance relations significantly.

Whether either of these developments, or some other outcome, occurs depends heavily on how U.S. and Chinese leaders deal with specific issues facing them. In general, the Clinton administration, along with other U.S. elites, has shown an evolving ability to differentiate among competing U.S. interests and to set goals that meet American needs and provide a basis for a more coherent approach to China than was evident in 1992-1995. The multifaceted challenges posed by China's rising power may call for the kind of strategy referred to as "conditional engagement" in a Council on Foreign Relations Study Group publication.[3]

The thrust of conditional engagement is to bring the PRC into the community of nations through China's acceptance of basic rules of international conduct. In general order of priority, those rules focus heavily first on military and security questions, notably opposition to PRC use of force against Taiwan or other countries and opposition to PRC proliferation of weapons of mass destruction and related technology; then economic issues such as access to the Chinese market, Chinese adherence to world IPR standards, labor practices, and related questions; and finally issues of values such as human rights and democracy.

The overall strategy of conditional engagement follows two parallel lines: economic engagement, to promote the integration of China into the global trading and financial systems; and security engagement, to encourage Chinese compliance with accepted international norms by diplomatic and military means when economic incentives do not suffice. Both are hedges against the risk of the emergence of a belligerent China. The strategy would require clear positive and negative incentives contained within U.S. policy, though how and when those incentives are used depend on circumstances.

The priorities of conditional engagement reflect a comprehensive assessment—arguably rare in U.S. policymaking—not only of what the United States cares about, but also of how much an issue weighs in overall U.S. national interests; how influential U.S. action may be in changing Chinese behavior; how best to elicit a desired Chinese response; and how to deal with effective Chinese defiance.

What is Beijing's likely response to a more coherent and better-understood set of U.S. policy priorities? On the one hand, Beijing clearly welcomes higher-level dialogue and U.S.-China summit meetings. Such interchange allows for communication among senior leaders that can clarify intentions and reduce misunderstandings. It sends signals to audiences at home and abroad that the Chinese leadership has emerged from the isolation imposed following the Tiananmen incident to a position of major prominence in world affairs. It also redounds to the credit of Chinese leaders like Jiang Zemin, who benefited from positive publicity associated with such summit meetings in the period surrounding the Chinese leadership's 15th Party Congress in 1997.

Meanwhile, an agenda of conditional engagement might set priorities more compatible with recent Chinese goals than recent U.S. policy has shown. Thus, for example, Chinese leaders were strongly resistant to U.S. efforts in the early Clinton administration to make human rights the defining issue in U.S.-China relations. They reportedly judged that giving in to U.S. pressures on this issue would concede sovereign weakness and invite more political opposition at home and abroad, threatening the communist party's monopoly of political power in China. In contrast, Beijing leaders were prepared to engage in the give-and-take of negotiations regarding U.S.-Chinese disputes over trade issues, questions of weapons proliferation, and other so-called nonsovereignty questions.

The main exception in the recent move toward greater compatibility concerns Taiwan. Although Beijing is prepared to speak flexibly in discussion with the United States and others over its right to use force in many areas, it remains resistant to any efforts to curb China's ability to use force in areas claimed by Beijing, especially Taiwan. Notably, the Clinton administration's willingness to deploy carrier battle groups in the face of Chinese intimidation of Taiwan demonstrates the seriousness of U.S. intent to curb PRC use of military force in this sensitive area.

For a time in early 1997, it appeared that the Clinton administration's greater attention to, and clearer priorities about, China policy and the generally positive PRC response would pave the way to substantial progress in U.S.-China relations prior to the summit meeting late in the year. Press reports discussed possible U.S.-China agreements on China's entry into the WTO, U.S. provision of permanent MFN treatment for China, human rights issues, and nuclear cooperation.[4]

In Congress, there also appeared to be growing support for the administration's stance. Scores of members traveled to China in the period between the end of the 104th Congress in 1996 and the start of the 105th in 1997. Many indicated that they were impressed by the vibrant Chinese economy and the potential for U.S. business there. The Chinese government continued to emphasize its determination to improve relations with Congress. It beefed up its embassy staff dealing with Congress from four to ten and appointed a new director for congressional relations who was Western educated and familiar with U.S. politics. Later disclosures also pointed to the influence China gained from legal and alleged illegal financial support for U.S. advocacy groups and politicians at this time. In general, such support, if true, acted to supplement an already vigorous Chinese effort to broaden and deepen Beijing's appeal in U.S. politics.

As time went on, critics of the administration's policy from both left and right launched often strident attacks. They were aided by a generally sympathetic U.S. media inclined to criticize the Chinese government and the Clinton administration's engagement policy. Also important, media disclosures linked an ongoing controversy over campaign fundraising by

President Clinton, Vice President Al Gore, and others to U.S. and foreign entities allegedly seeking to use campaign donations in order to encourage smooth U.S.-China relations. In Congress, the disclosures had the effect of dampening somewhat congressional enthusiasm for visits to China sponsored by Chinese organizations or organizations with an interest in U.S.-China relations. Chinese officials noted that the political atmosphere in Washington in spring 1997 complicated their recently stepped-up efforts to lobby in Congress, but they judged that they would continue efforts to build closer ties with Congress over the long term.[5]

In spring 1997, President Clinton and Vice President Gore adopted a notably lower posture in defense of their China policy. In part this stance appeared designed to limit the political damage stemming from charges that they had been influenced by pro-China campaign contributions. While waiting for the political controversy to subside, the president and vice president presumably judged that Beijing would take no unusual action contrary to past practice that might undermine U.S.-China relations. Thus, there was little likelihood that diminished public support of China policy from the White House would lead to PRC retaliation.[6]

However, the lower White House profile did open the door to U.S. critics of the policy. This set the stage for a congressional debate on MFN in 1997 more heated than in recent years. Partisans on both the left and the right used China-related issues for domestic political reasons. Thus, some Democrats who opposed Gore as the prospective party nominee in 2000 used these issues to discredit the vice president. At the same time, some in Republican ranks pressed the same issues to force Republican leaders to pay more attention to the policy agenda favored by social conservatives.

MFN was sustained for another year by the House on June 24, 1997. In particular, the vote showed the power of the business lobby and business interests to offset the more vigorous lobbying effort of the wide range of U.S. critics of China's policies and practices. On this key issue, business interests weighed in heavily in support of continued MFN treatment for China, including a letter to the House speaker signed by over 1,000 U.S. companies.[7]

Despite renewal of MFN, the net effect of the vigorous policy debate was to dampen prospects for forward movement in U.S.-China relations, at least for the time being. In particular, the media actively continued to debate China issues. Major legislation in Congress was honeycombed with important measures targeted at China's policies and practices. A highlight of Senate hearings on campaign-finance irregularities was the charge that China allegedly used illegal donations to sway U.S. politicians and policy.

The Washington Summit,
October 1997—Expectations and Outcome

In the two months leading up to Chinese President Jiang Zemin's official summit meetings with President Clinton in Washington, D.C., on October 28-29, 1997, White House, State Department, and Defense Department officials were actively briefing academic, think tank, and congressional audiences on a not-for-attribution basis on their motives and expectations.[8]

U.S. Motives

Administration officers sought to use the summit to strengthen an ongoing process of Sino-American contacts and negotiations, a process that over time would establish frameworks and institutions for integrating China's rising power and influence into the "web" of international norms. China was seen at a crossroads, especially after the death of Deng Xiaoping earlier in the year and the conclusion of the 15th Chinese Party Congress in September. According to U.S. officials, Chinese leaders remained divided over whether to respond positively to international opportunities and commitments. Jiang Zemin and Vice Premier Zhu Rongji were seen as leaning in a positive direction but meeting some resistance from such leaders as Premier Li Peng and officers in the Chinese military, who were depicted as more inward looking and nationalistic.

In the U.S. officials' view, U.S. policy and actions would influence this debate in China. It was seen by the administration to be in U.S. interests to encourage the outward, positive leanings of Chinese leaders and use the opportunity of the summit to reinforce China's integration into the international community and adherence to international norms. Some Clinton administration briefers argued that Chinese leaders are inclined to respond positively to the U.S. efforts if only because they have a deeper appreciation recently of American staying power in the post-cold war period. In this view, Chinese leaders for a time after the end of the cold war anticipated a decline in U.S. strength and the emergence of a multipolar world where rising China would exert ever-greater influence. In fact, the judgment went, the United States was growing even stronger and more influential in the post-cold war period, and thus it was in China's interests to avoid confrontation with the sole remaining superpower and to establish a constructive working relationship with Washington.

The means to build this kind of Sino-U.S. relationship of greater cooperation and trust revolved around high-level discussion of respective foreign and defense policy interests and objectives—the so-called strategic dialogue. Since 1996, the Clinton administration and Chinese counterparts had been particularly focused on these kinds of in-depth exchanges, according to White House briefers. As one official put it, "Whenever we get together with the Chinese, we start with a discussion of foreign and security issues." Another maintained that this dialogue had led to a major change in high-level U.S.-China interaction: the two sides no longer saw one another as adversaries and were able to develop a good deal of meaningful common ground on important international questions. The dialogue also built a certain degree of mutual trust, which allowed the Sino-U.S. relationship to develop to a point that it no longer hinged on the outcome of a sensitive individual dispute, as often had been the case in the recent past.

U.S. Expectations

Administration briefers sometimes advised that the summit would not produce any big concessions or gestures by one side or the other. Rather, they stressed that the summit was part of an ongoing process moving through many channels and over several years to achieve the objectives described earlier. At other times, however, the briefers made clear that both the U.S. and Chinese administrations were mustering a range of evidence of progress on issues both sides had been working on over the past year. The governments could showcase such progress at the meeting or in subsequent exchanges leading to the reciprocal Sino-U.S. summit scheduled for Beijing in 1998. Indeed, administration officials emphasized that they were using the opportunity to press the Chinese to make commitments that would be cited as progress or so-called "deliverables." They argued that a top-level meeting without these tangible agreements would be seen by many in the United States as one-sided. It would give the Chinese leaders their main objective—i.e., the legitimacy and political status that flow from such high-level treatment by the United States—but it would be seen by critics as offering little concrete benefit on issues of importance for the United States.

The Eight "Baskets of Deliverables." Administration briefers sometimes divided these clusters of issues under negotiation between the three "hard ones" and five others. The former were of keenest concern to many in Congress, the U.S. media, and elsewhere—i.e., China's proliferation of weapons of mass destruction and related technology and delivery systems, trade issues, and human rights.

- Proliferation. Administration officials averred that they were working very hard with China on issues of nuclear proliferation to produce arrangements and assurances that would allow the president to certify China's compliance with international safeguards and thereby open the way for implementation of the long-delayed U.S.-China nuclear cooperation agreement. They cited a range of recently enacted Chinese laws and regulations restricting China's nuclear-related exports in ways sought by the United States. They noted ongoing U.S. concerns about Chinese activities with Pakistan and Iran but judged that progress was being made here as well. Briefers differed on the likelihood of U.S. certification in time for the Clinton-Jiang summit, with some expressing optimism that agreement could be reached and others pessimistic that the president would issue certification in the current circumstances. Administration briefers were less upbeat about progress in promoting Chinese adherence to international norms regarding chemical-weapons technology and missile systems, but the administration was pressing Beijing in these areas as well.

- Trade. Despite protracted Sino-U.S. negotiations and a flurry of high-level economic visitors to Beijing, administration briefers were not optimistic about quick progress over issues involving China's entry into the World Trade Organization (WTO). Some suggested China might be pursuing a strategy of reaching separate agreements on WTO with Japan, Australia, and the European Union (EU) as a way of outflanking the United States but added that this would be a "big miscalculation" on Beijing's part. Administration briefers held out the possibility that enough progress might be made on WTO issues to allow for a "down payment"—a partial agreement in time for the summit. They said this in turn might prompt President Clinton to reaffirm his commitment to work for China's WTO entry and to announce at the same time his intention to grant permanent most-favored-nation tariff status for China once the PRC gets into the WTO on terms acceptable to the United States.

- Human Rights. Administration officials did not expect the Chinese leaders to focus on possible movement in the sensitive area of human rights until after the 15th Party Congress in September 1997. They continued to press the Chinese hard on this issue, noting that progress here would have a greater impact on U.S. attitudes toward the Chinese government than most other issues. In general, the administration was pressing for release of dissidents; Chinese agreement to the two UN covenants on human rights; access by the Red Cross and other international monitors to Chinese prisons; and accounting for Chinese prisoners. Some administration briefers were optimistic that Chinese leaders would make significant gestures on these issues in time for the summit, while others were more noncommittal.

- Defense. Progress here would include an accord dealing with "incidents at sea," greater military-to-military exchanges, coordination of Sino-U.S. military involvement in humanitarian efforts overseas, and some possible progress on safety issues related to nuclear weapons. Briefers maintained that the U.S. side was interested in an accord on mutual de-targeting of nuclear weapons, but China had set a precondition that the United States and China must first agree to a no-first-use principle regarding nuclear weapons—something the United States has long opposed.

- Law Enforcement/Rule of Law. The United States was seeking closer ties with China to combat international terrorism and was seeking reciprocal visits leading to a possible framework being established for mutual legal assistance. The Drug Enforcement Agency might be able to reach agreement on establishing an office in China, but according to administration officials, it appeared that an FBI office in China was not in the offing. High-level exchanges and mutual visits were expected to flesh out a Rule of Law initiative recently launched under the direction of Professor Paul Gwertz on detail to the State Department.

- Energy and Environment. There were active exchanges by the vice president's office and the State Department, among others, during the weeks prior to the summit. Focal points included possible accords and exchanges on clean-coal technology, rural electrification, and climate change.

- Science and Technology. Exchanges and accords here would try to consolidate the variety of U.S.-China arrangements in these areas. New initiatives could involve space technology and expanded U.S. Fulbright support for Chinese-U.S. expert exchanges.

- Strategic Consultation. Anticipated agreements and understanding would broaden existing exchanges between foreign policy leaders to include cabinet-level and lower-level consultations with relevant State Department, Defense Department, and other strategic-policy leaders. This "basket" also included a U.S. effort to get China to pay more of UN expenses as the United States sought to lower its allotment to the world body. The two sides would also establish a hot line for communication during crises.

China's Motives

In addition to the international prestige and status that accompany a visit to the United States, administration briefers noted that China was seeking several actions from the United States, notably:

- Strong affirmation of existing U.S. commitments on Taiwan. The briefers pointed out that there would be no fourth communiqué to follow the three Sino-U.S. communiqués on Taiwan issued since 1972. They also believed that the United States could continue its current pattern of arms sales to Taiwan without endangering U.S.-Chinese relations.

- Stronger administration efforts to block current legislation critical of China that was pending before the 105th Congress.
- Ending U.S. sanctions in place since the 1989 Tiananmen incident that block the Overseas Private Investment Corporation and the Trade and Development Agency from working in China. Depending on progress on human rights and proliferation questions, China also sought a halt to U.S. efforts to bring China's human rights record before the UN Human Rights Commission and a consummation of the U.S.-China nuclear energy agreement.

The briefers were forthright in voicing their view that current congressional legislation that was critical of China seriously complicated the administration's approach to the summit. By early October, administration briefers were cautiously optimistic that most of such legislation would not see floor action until after the meeting. They also noted that the administration was working to keep Taipei fully briefed on the implications of the summit for Taiwan interests and that the Taipei government seemed satisfied with the outlook. One briefer pointedly noted that Jiang Zemin and his entourage were paying close attention to the protocol treatment they were to receive, comparing it to that accorded Deng Xiaoping during his visit to Washington in 1979. They noted that they had advised the Chinese to pay more attention to the substance of the visit and less to the form.

Outcome and Outlook

After the summit, administration briefers predictably accentuated the positive in what was widely seen as mixed results.[9] From the U.S. side, the major achievement focused on progress on nuclear issues. Specifically, the administration agreed to certify China's practices in the area of nuclear proliferation according to existing U.S. law, thereby opening the way to implementation of a U.S.-PRC nuclear-cooperation agreement signed in 1985. Under U.S. law, Congress has thirty legislative days to overrule the president's certification with a two-thirds vote. The administration acted after China took several important steps to bring its nuclear-transfer policies in line with international norms and to end all nuclear cooperation with Iran.

President Clinton voiced satisfaction with U.S.-China strategic dialogue and cooperation seen at the summit. He especially noted China's role as a participant in the four-party (South and North Korea in addition to the

United States and China) talks on seeking peace on the Korean peninsula.

Jiang Zemin strongly defended Chinese positions on the Tiananmen incident, Tibet, and political and religious freedom. Beijing refrained from releasing any political dissidents at the time of the summit, although leading dissident Wei Jingsheng was released on medical parole to the United States two weeks after Jiang returned home from his U.S. trip. Some headway was made in getting the Chinese authorities to account for political prisoners and to engage in dialogue and allow site visits by U.S. and other human rights groups.

Progress on economic issues was disappointing, especially when compared to the expectations on WTO and permanent MFN noted earlier in the year. China agreed to participate in the International Technology Agreement, thereby presumably seeking to cut Chinese tariffs on computers and telecommunications equipment. An official Chinese buying mission, concurrent with Jiang Zemin's visit, announced the purchase of over $4 billion of U.S. goods, mostly Boeing aircraft.

Progress in other areas also was mixed. In defense, the incidents-at-sea accord and agreement on exchanges were endorsed, but not joint humanitarian exercises nor de-targeting nuclear weapons. Legal exchanges moved forward, as did government-to-government cooperation on environmental, scientific, and energy issues.

The Chinese claimed to be satisfied with the U.S. public reassurances on Taiwan. Chinese media said U.S. officials went into greater detail in private, specifically ruling out U.S. support for Taiwan independence.[10] The Clinton administration worked with House leaders to delay consideration of nine bills with provisions critical of China until after Jiang Zemin left Washington. However, the bills were considered and passed by wide margins in the House immediately thereafter.[11] President Clinton decided not to end the remaining U.S. sanctions on economic interaction with China stemming from the Tiananmen incident, except for the one related to U.S. nuclear cooperation with China. Jiang Zemin's strong defense of China's human rights policies and practices was matched by President Clinton's opposition to those policies. U.S. officials did not refer to any possible change in the annual efforts to bring China's record before the UN Human Rights Commission.

Jiang Zemin left the United States in early November and spent the next two months in high-level summitry with Boris Yeltsin and Russian leaders in Beijing; Asian and Pacific leaders at the Asian Pacific Economic Cooperation (APEC) meeting in Vancouver; Canadian and Mexican leaders in their countries; and the Association of Southeast Asian Nations (ASEAN) and other Asian leaders meeting in Kuala Lumpur. Throughout, Jiang and his entourage, echoed by PRC media, hailed the "complete success" of his summit with President Clinton. They saw the improved Sino-U.S. relationship as reaching a "new historical stage" where the "ups and downs" of recent years had ended in favor of concerted efforts by both sides to build a "constructive strategic partnership." Year-end PRC commentary depicted the improved relationship as the centerpiece of a matrix of recently established and enhanced Chinese partnerships and relationships with Russia, France, Japan, and other world powers designed to stabilize China's foreign-policy relations as Beijing focused on internal issues of economic reform.

U.S. leaders were more low-key after the summit. U.S. government observers were uncertain how the pull of competing interest groups and other factors would affect the U.S.-China relationship in 1998. On the one hand, it appeared clear that both leaderships were determined to build on the momentum of the October 1997 summit and whenever possible avoid actions that would undermine prospects for the Beijing summit in 1998. On the other hand, it appeared likely that the momentum would be challenged by events in the first half of 1998 driven by the congressional calendar and backed by the wide range of U.S. groups that remain actively critical of China. Thus, groups critical of China—led by those concerned by China's record or proliferation of weapons of mass destruction and related technology—were expected to work with sympathetic members of Congress at the outset of the second session of the 105th Congress in late January 1998. Their specific goal was to enact into law legislation passed by the House in 1997 that would give Congress 120 days to consider any presidential certification allowing U.S. nuclear cooperation with China. Current law gives Congress thirty days for consideration. The groups would then turn to halting the certification by publicizing, through congressional deliberations and sympathetic media, the evidence of China's past and recent weapons proliferation practice. Even if they fail to halt the certification and U.S.-China nuclear cooperation, as appeared likely, the critics endeavored to tarnish China's reputation among Americans and weaken support for U.S. policy.

American groups critical of China's human rights policies continued past practice and used the late-January release of the State Department's annual human rights report as an opportunity to press their case that China has done little to conform to international norms in this area. Groups critical of China over trade issues will probably follow past form in using the annual release of U.S. trade figures in February to prompt congressional hearings dealing with the rapid growth of the U.S. trade deficit with the PRC. Meanwhile, critics of China and others may use a new report to Congress, due in late February and mandated by the fiscal year 1998 intelligence authorization bill on Chinese spying in the United States, to expose Chinese activity in this sensitive area. As in the past, congressional critics, backed by a wide range of U.S. interest groups and supported by a U.S. media inclined to highlight negative features of Chinese government practices, are once again preparing to use the required annual presidential decision on MFN for China in order to publicize their views.

The incentives for the critics remain the same as in the recent past. In addition to sincere concern with Chinese policies and practices, some use China-related issues for partisan and other reasons. Partisan motives likely will grow in 1998—an election year. Meanwhile, congressional critics see few immediate negative consequences for their actions. Thus, while they are hailed by sympathetic interest groups and media, neither the Chinese government nor the Clinton administration takes significant steps to sanction or otherwise punish them for opposing the avowed policy of engagement.

In sum, congressional critics, for the time being at least, can view their criticism of China as a "free ride." Under current circumstances, it is unlikely to lead to a substantial negative change in U.S. policy. Rather, it establishes a negative atmosphere that creates a drag on U.S. and PRC administration efforts to move the U.S.-China relationship forward.

The 1997-1998 Asian economic crisis and the U.S. confrontation with Iraq over UN weapons inspections diverted U.S. attention from China and, for a time at least, reduced criticism of China in Congress and the media. Meanwhile, the 1996-1997 allegations of illegal Chinese government funding of U.S. political campaigns failed to generate much interest in 1998 after a period of active congressional and media scrutiny the previous year. Critics were unable to link China conclusively to significant illegal payments or other illegal activities. Investigations by a House committee and the Department of Justice continued. It appeared that the issue would remain of secondary importance in the coming year unless major new disclosures were to occur.

Implications for the Future

The recent movement toward greater clarity of priorities and coherence in Clinton administration policy toward China remains tentative. Many forces in both countries are at odds with recent trends leading toward higher-level U.S.-China meetings. Those forces may rise to greater prominence if U.S. and Chinese leaders falter in their efforts to broaden common ground and deal constructively with their many differences. In any event, friction in U.S.-China relations could increase over such possible developments as tensions over Taiwan, Hong Kong's reversion to PRC control, a major crackdown on political dissent in China, or weapons proliferation, to name only a few possibilities.

Under such circumstances, U.S. organized interests should have many opportunities to influence policy. Using access to Congress, and having the support of the media to focus on China's infractions of U.S.-backed international norms, interest groups critical of the Chinese government would have ample occasion to shift policy in their direction. Their effectiveness would depend heavily on their ability to mobilize active support, clarify and amplify their message, exploit entry points into the policy process in Congress or elsewhere, and adopt a proper balance in dealing with both supporters and skeptics among policymakers. At the same time, U.S. groups favoring a smoother relationship with the Chinese government would also remain comparably active and attentive in order to protect their interests.

U.S. leaders would presumably continue to play the "two-level game" prevailing in foreign affairs; that is, they would pursue policies that not only deal effectively with China and its leaders in an international setting but also manage the variety of active, organized interests in the United States. Faced with uncertainty over China's future and a continued tug-of-war among often-competing organized groups at home, U.S. leaders may well have a hard time arriving at a consistent and coherent approach to the PRC. Recent experience in U.S.-China policy suggests that consistent policy under these circumstances may be the exception rather than the rule.

A different set of implications for organized interests flows from a strengthening of the recent tentative movement toward clarity of priorities and coherence in U.S. policy toward China. If U.S. policymakers increasingly converge in their view of the great importance of managing relations with a rising China, this could place policy in a category of "strategic policy." Thus, China would be seen as a major power capable of prompting serious crises affecting basic U.S. interests, comparable to the emergency in the Taiwan area in early 1996. As we discussed earlier, John Tierney and other scholars argue that such circumstances usually lessen the opportunity for organized interests opposed to prevailing policy to exert their influence. As a consequence, organized interests pressing the United States to adopt strong confrontational policies may find their power reduced. Examples include those who favor Taiwan or Tibetan independence or those who would make China's handling of political dissent the ultimate litmus test.

Tierney and others note that, as the rise of China gains high visibility and acceptance among U.S. leaders, the ability of organized interests to prompt U.S. government actions at odds with public positions is reduced. These groups may find, however, that they are better able to exert influence behind the scenes in low-visibility policy areas. A case in point is pro-Taiwan lobbying since the crisis of 1995-1996. Recognizing that Taipei has little to gain and perhaps much to lose from pushing for further support of Taiwan's international status at a time of highly visible interaction between the United States and PRC, the Taiwan government and supporting organized interests in the United States have reverted to a low-key posture. They have focused instead on nurturing the positive view and goodwill toward Taiwan that resulted from the March 1996 presidential elections, using widespread but unobstrusive contacts, meetings, conferences, and other diplomatic and informational means. These efforts also have included initiatives for building greater trust between the U.S. and Taiwan administrations after the friction caused by the Lee Teng-hui visit. With this increased trust, Taipei would be able to gain better access to U.S. administration officials while retaining close ties to Congress, the media, and others.

Greater coherence and convergence of opinion among U.S. elites regarding U.S.-China policy clearly assist the efforts of organized interests whose goals are compatible with that policy. For example, recent Clinton administration priorities appear to conform substantially with the goals of business lobbyists who want to avoid major economic sanctions against China. Some of these organized interests are now encouraging policymakers to remove the legislative requirement for an annual presidential waiver so that China will receive permanent MFN tariff treatment. They argue that this would quell a major irritant and uncertainty in U.S.-Chinese economic relations and avoid repetition of the acrimonious congressional debates on China conducted monthly since 1990.[12]

This recent movement toward greater coherence and convergence in China policy does little to reduce the difficulty organized interests have in *initiating* national policy. Although it is hard to argue with the success of business interests in helping to block the application of human rights and other conditions on MFN for China, scholarship shows that it is much more difficult for such interests, even under favorable political circumstances, to initiate new policy. Changing the MFN procedures for China would appear to represent such an initiative, and therefore could be more difficult than merely ensuring that MFN tariff treatment is not withdrawn. Not only would popular and media opinion probably be skeptical of such a move, but congressional desire to keep the existing provision in order to exert influence on the PRC and U.S.-China policy remains strong.

Whether U.S. policy continues to be subject to tugs-of-war among competing U.S. organized interests or follows a pattern of a strategic orientation with clearer and more coherent priorities, we can assess the balance in the two levels (international and national) influencing U.S. foreign policy. In particular, if U.S. leaders focus on building a constructive relationship with China's leaders in the international context, without paying enough attention to domestic concerns, they run the risk of being attacked effectively as was George Bush over his consistent policy toward China. If they tilt to U.S. domestic pressures, as President Clinton did in reversing policy and offering a visa to Lee Teng-hui, they could prompt a dangerous crisis with an increasingly powerful China.

We can draw some important lessons from this recent experience for

U.S. policymakers:

• earlier and more extensive consultation with relevant interest groups,
• engagement with these groups over policy at an early stage, not just after a policy has been formed, and
• an awareness of how public and interest-group opinion on policy issues could change, and formulating policies in ways that would take account of such change.

Although consultation normally is politically prudent in a government of divided powers, following the prevailing consensus among U.S. organized interests may not lead to good policy. The model of the two-level game emphasizes that strategic policies cannot be divorced from U.S. domestic interests, but that they also must accord with the role of the United States in world affairs.

Notes

1. This section is based heavily on Robert Sutter, *China's Rising Power: Alternative U.S. National Security Strategies—Findings of a Seminar*, CRS Report 96-518F, June 6, 1996. See also CRS Memorandum to Congressional China Watchers, dated August 8, 1996.
2. For background on this recent trend in U.S. thinking, see Robert Sutter, *China's Rising Power: Alternative U.S. National Security Strategies*, CRS Report 96-518F, June 6, 1996.
3. James Shinn, ed., *Weaving the Net: Conditional Engagement with China* (New York: Council on Foreign Relations, 1996).
4. See review in *Congressional Quarterly Weekly Report* (June 28, 1997): 1536-37.
5. Interviews January 2, 1997, Washington, D.C. Interviews May 30, 1997, Beijing.
6. Some observers speculated as well that the president and his advisers may have judged that the partisan debate over China policy would exacerbate difficulties for Speaker Newt Gingrich, who generally supported MFN for China but faced challenges from other Republicans supportive of social conservatives critical of China. Thus, by adopting a low profile, the White House allowed the arena of dispute to focus on the House of Representatives, where the China policy debate was likely to increase differences among Republicans and perhaps make it easier for the Democrats to regain control of the House in 1998. (Interviews, Washington, D.C., June 1997.)
7. *Congressional Record* (June 24, 1997): H 4281.
8. The presentations were given in academic and think tank settings in the Washington, D.C., area during late September and early October 1997. For a good discussion, see David Shambaugh, *The 1997 Sino-American Summit*, Asian Update, The Asia Society, October 1997.

9. Department of State press guidance, October 31, 1997. See U.S. press coverage giving mixed assessments of summit results.

10. Xinhua coverage of Foreign Minister Qian Qichan press conference, October 29, 1997.

11. *Washington Post*, October 30, 1997; *Congressional Record*, November 6, 7, 1997.

12. See notably CRS Memorandum to Congressional China Watchers, dated October 24, 1996.

Appendix

Organized Groups with Current Interests in U.S. Policy toward China

What follows is a brief listing of some of the organized groups that have shown an interest in U.S. policy toward China in recent years. Except where noted the information included under each organization was provided by that organization in writing or by telephone contact during preparation of this study. Information noted in quotation marks below is taken directly from written information provided by the organization. This listing is not comprehensive. It is provided to give readers a reference to some of the organizations referred to in the text.

AFL-CIO

A federation of eighty-six unions, the AFL-CIO represents about 75 percent of U.S. organized labor.

Comment

The federation has had an active program critical of China over human rights abuses, especially labor rights and use of prison labor. The support of the federation and its long-standing expertise at lobbying and at influencing executive-branch and congressional decisionmakers have made it an important force on the side of those criticizing and urging trade restrictions and sanctions against China.

The American Assembly (of Columbia University)

Founded: 1950

Focus on China: Recently active with several projects dealing with China policy.

Purpose and Scope: An affiliate of Columbia University, the American Assembly is a national, educational institution incorporated in the state of New York. The American Assembly seeks to provide information, stimulate discussion, and evoke independent conclusions on matters of vital public interest.

Primary Goals

American Assembly Sessions. At least two national assembly programs are initiated each year. Authorities are retained to write background papers presenting data and defining the main issues of each subject. Programs dealing with U.S. China policy have been prominent in recent years. A group of men and women representing a broad range of experience, competence, and American leadership meet for several days to discuss the assembly topic and consider alternatives for national policy.

All assemblies follow essentially the same procedure. The background papers are sent to participants in advance of the assembly. The assembly meets in small groups for four or five lengthy periods. All groups use the same agenda. At the close of these informal sessions, participants adopt in plenary session a final report of findings and recommendations. Regional, state, and local assemblies are held following the national session at Arden House. Assemblies have also been held in England, Switzerland, Malaysia, Canada, the Caribbean, South America, Central America, the Philippines, and Japan. Over 160 institutions have cosponsored one or more assemblies.

Positions on China and Taiwan

The American Assembly takes no position on U.S. China policy issues.

Comment

American Assembly forums and publications tend to endorse views that favor a carefully balanced U.S. policy toward China that continues MFN treatment and avoids changes in U.S.-Taiwan relations that would upset overall U.S.-China relations.

American Enterprise Institute
for Public Policy Research (AEI)

Founded: 1943
Focus on China: Included in the Asian studies section of Foreign and Defense Policy Studies.
Membership/Area of Influence: AEI promotes public policy research through books, scholarly journals, congressional testimony, lectures, conferences and papers. AEI's home office is in Washington, D.C.
Activities: Educational, public policy research.
Funding: AEI is a nonpartisan, nonprofit organization that derives its financial support from private, corporate, and foundation donations plus money generated from conferences and sales.
Annual Budget: 1993 expenses totaled $11,747,402.
Phone: (202) 862-5800 *Fax:* (202) 862-7178

Primary Goals

AEI was created to research economic policy, which remains its primary if not sole objective today. AEI research aims to preserve and strengthen the foundations of a free society—limited government, competitive private enterprise, vital cultural and political institutions, and vigilant defense, through rigorous inquiry, debate and writing. Today AEI research extends beyond economic policy to include Foreign and Defense Policy Studies and Social and Political Studies. Topics relating to U.S.-China relations can be found in the three sections, ranging from political and military relationships to economic and trade issues to legal studies. Although China studies are not a priority at AEI, China receives substantial coverage, through the areas noted above, with Foreign and Defense Policy Studies providing most of the research. AEI is nonpartisan in its research.

Positions on China and Taiwan

As a nonpartisan research institute, AEI has no political position on China or Taiwan.

Comment

Under the leadership of Thomas Robinson and James Lilley, AEI sponsored a number of important studies and seminars that argued strongly for a balanced U.S. policy toward China that would support continued MFN treatment for China. The programs also supported active U.S. engagement with Taiwan.

Amnesty International

Founded: 1961
Focus on China: Among many others.
Membership/Area of Influence: 1.1 million members in 150 countries and territories. The largest human rights organization in the world with 320 paid staff members, AI has regional offices in the United States in Los Angeles; San Francisco; Somerville, Massachusetts; Atlanta; Chicago; and Washington, D.C.
Activities: Educational (human rights), political.
Funding: Amnesty International is funded through donations in order to maintain its position as an impartial research source. Amnesty International does employ professional fundraisers to generate support.
Annual Budget: NA.
Phone: (202) 775-5161 *Fax:* (202) 775-5992

Primary Goals

Amnesty International is dedicated to the preservation and widening of human rights around the world. Its mandate is based on the United Nations' Universal Declaration of Human Rights of 1948. Amnesty's main focus is to "free all prisoners of conscience. These are people detained anywhere for their beliefs or because of their ethnic origin, sex, color, or language—who have not used or advocated violence; ensure fair and prompt trials for political prisoners; abolish the death penalty, torture and other cruel inhuman or degrading treatment of prisoners; end extrajudicial executions and 'disappearances'; oppose abuses by opposition groups including hostage taking, torture and deliberate and arbitrary killings; and prevent degrading treatment or punishment of all prisoners."

Position on China

"Amnesty is impartial. It does not support or oppose any government or political system. It believes human rights must be respected universally. It takes up cases whenever it considers there are reliable grounds for concern, regardless of the ideology of the government, or the beliefs of the victim. Human rights transcends national boundaries. This principle has been recognized by the world's main inter-governmental organizations. . . . Amnesty seeks observance of the human rights standards that governments themselves have adopted internationally."

Comment

Amnesty International does not take positions on U.S. policy issues such as whether or not to extend MFN treatment to China. The thrust of its research and interest, however, clearly affects the U.S. political atmosphere in ways that argue against MFN treatment for China. In particular, it highlights continued widespread Chinese government human rights violations, giving strength to the arguments of those in the United States calling for a cutoff of MFN for China.

Activities

Although Amnesty International has been interested in human rights abuses in China for some time, in March 1996 AI launched a new China human rights campaign, entitled "China—No One Is Safe (Political repression and abuse of power in the 1990s)." Amnesty has emphasized its focus and efforts in China to promote human rights, and is concerned primarily with the following issues:

- Death Penalty—Amnesty reports that capital punishment is used more in China than in the rest of the world combined, and that executions often take place in public following an unfair trial.
- Torture—Amnesty opposes China's use of torture, which includes severe beatings, the use of electric batons, prolonged use of handcuffs, and whippings.
- Abuse of Power—China is accused of misusing state and local government power to punish those who are seen as challenging to the government. Misuses include trumped-up charges, excessive penalties for minor infractions, and trials with predetermined outcomes.
- Political Dissidents—China has arrested hundreds of people for simply calling for political reform.
- Labor Activists—Workers may join only the All-China Federation of Trade Unions, which is sponsored by the government. All other trade unions are illegal, and organizers will be arrested.
- Human Rights Defenders—People campaigning for human rights have been arrested and charged with being counterrevolutionaries.
- Religious Groups—Amnesty opposes China's ban on religious freedom and the arrests of people for practicing unauthorized religions.
- Regional Repression—People in several regions have been victims of serious human rights violations in connection with demands for political independence or respect of cultural identity.
- Birth Control Policy—China has enforced compulsory birth control

since 1979 and enforces a quota system. Women who have more than the legally allowed number of children are forced to have abortions or undergo sterilization procedures.

To generate support for the campaign, Amnesty International has outlined a strategy for both the Chinese government and the international community to follow. Amnesty hopes that through international and domestic pressure, China's government will move to correct the above areas of human rights contention. Through lobbying, protests, and the distribution of publications, Amnesty hopes to persuade the international community to act on the following initiatives:

- Encourage the Chinese government to ratify international human rights treaties and to invite UN human rights experts and relevant human rights organizations to visit China to investigate human rights.
- Whenever possible, open up dialogue with the Chinese authorities on human rights issues and exert pressure on them to conform to international human rights norms.
- Use every opportunity when developing cultural or economic links with Chinese people to create a common understanding of human rights.
- Ensure that no security equipment is transferred to China where there is reason to believe that such equipment will contribute to arbitrary detentions, torture, or ill treatment.

Asia Foundation

Focus on China: Entire existence.
Purpose and Scope: The Asia Foundation receives U.S. government funding as well as support from nongovernment sources. It supports a wide range of exchanges, research, conferences, and other U.S.-Asian interchanges.

Comment

The Asia Foundation has been a key element in U.S. interaction with Asia for many decades. It avoids taking positions on controversial policy questions. Its trustees include scholars such as Robert Scalapino and Harry Harding, who are closely identified with a carefully balanced U.S. policy toward China, continued MFN treatment for China, and a moderate U.S. stance toward Taiwan that avoids upsetting U.S.-mainland China relations. Its many publications include *America's Role in Asia* (1993), urging a constructive U.S. policy of interaction with mainland China.

Asia-Pacific Exchange Foundation
(Formerly Far East Studies Institute)

Founded: 1980s
Focus on China: Entire existence.
Purpose and Scope: Since the 1980s, the group has arranged a number of congressional member and staff delegations to China each year. It works with both the House and the Senate. It has good access to Chinese foreign policy institutes that in turn provide access to Chinese officials of interest to the congressional visitors.

Comment

The purpose of the visits is to build mutual understanding. As such, they promote a U.S. policy encouraging closer cooperation with China, continued MFN treatment, and avoiding enhanced U.S. ties with Taiwan that would seriously complicate U.S.-mainland China relations.

The Asia Society

Founded: 1956
Focus on China: Entire existence.
Membership/Area of Influence: The Asia Society has an administrative staff of eighty-five people, but through its publications, seminars, and conferences it is able to reach an international audience. The Asia Society has branch offices in Hong Kong, Houston, Los Angeles, and Washington, D.C.
Activities: Educational.
Publications: Asian Updates, China Briefing, India Briefing, Korea Briefing
Funding: The Asia Society is funded through foundation and corporate grants and contributions, program service fees, membership, special events, individual contributions, contributed services, and endowments. In 1996, the Asia Society did not accept contract research. The Asia Society currently has assets of $34,450,120.
Annual Budget: $9,951,625.
Phone: (212) 288-6400 *Fax:* (212) 517-8315

Primary Goals

"The Asia Society is America's leading institution dedicated to fostering understanding of Asia and communication between Americans and the peoples of Asia and the Pacific. The Society provides a forum for building awareness of the more than thirty countries broadly defined as the

Asia-Pacific region—the area from Japan to Iran, and from Russia to New Zealand, Australia, and the Pacific Islands. Through art exhibitions and performances, seminars and conferences, publications and assistance to the media, and materials and programs for students and teachers, the Asia Society presents the richness and diversity of Asia to the American people." The mandate of the Asia Society is to "build bridges of understanding between Americans and Asians."

Activities

In working toward its goal of creating understanding and awareness between Americans and Asians, the Asia Society is involved in a wide range of activities. In the United States, the Asia Society produces and provides multimedia curricular materials and informational services to schools throughout the country. "Video letters" depicting life in Asia from the perspective of Asian students have been created, allowing elementary and secondary school children to understand their Asian counterparts better. Coupled with the materials provided for students are programs that sponsor teacher training to better allow educators to assist students in understanding Asia. Additionally, the Asia Society maintains a national resource center with materials devoted to teaching about Asia.

For adults, the Asia Society sponsors study missions, conferences, and public programs on a wide range of Asian topics throughout the United States so that the United States and Asian nations can examine critical policy questions on U.S.-Asia relations. The Asia Society has conducted studies on security policies toward China and a lecture series on Chinese political and cultural life before and after the Tiananmen incident. Also, the Asia Society hosts the annual Williamsburg Conference, which allows leaders from business, academia, the media, and government to meet in a productive environment.

To reach a wider audience, the Asia Society uses the media, various publications, and television to encourage better understanding of Asia. The "films" program of the Asia Society screens Asian feature films and documentaries. The Asia Society publishes biannual briefings on China, India, and Korea, with background papers being published on a range of topics concerning Asia. Some examples of China-related research include "Issues in U.S. Relations with the Asia and the Pacific," "Brothers in Arms: Political Struggle and Competition in Taiwan's Evolving Democracy," "The Rule of Old Men in China: Policy Issues and Prospects for the Future," and "The 1989 Taiwan Elections."

Positions on China and Taiwan

The Asia Society, a nonprofit, nonpolitical organization, does not have a defined position on Chinese/Taiwanese issues.

Comment

Historically very active on China-related issues, the Asia Society has also shown some interest in Taiwan. Its forums and publications are seen by some to favor a balanced U.S. policy toward China, continued U.S. MFN treatment for China, and avoidance of change in U.S. policy toward Taiwan that would jeopardize U.S.-PRC relations. The Asia Society itself carefully avoids taking sides on such questions.

The Atlantic Council of the United States

Founded: 1961
Focus on China: Included in Program on Atlantic-Pacific Interrelationships.
Membership/Area of Influence: The Atlantic Council promotes public policy research and related programs addressing the advancement of U.S. interests engaged in the issues before the Atlantic and Pacific communities.
Activities: Educational, public policy research.
Funding: The Atlantic Council is a nonpartisan, nonprofit organization that receives financial support from foundations, corporations, individual donors, and the U.S. government.
Annual Budget: $2,375,000 (1994).
Phone: (202) 463-7226 *Fax:* (202) 463-7240

Primary Goals and Activities

The Atlantic Council seeks to advance U.S. global interests through analysis, prescription, and education. A national, nonpartisan organization, the Atlantic Council actively engages the U.S. executive and legislative branches, the national and international business communities, media and academics, and diplomats and other foreign leaders. Council programs identify issues and opportunities, highlight choices, foster informed public debate, and provide education about American foreign, security, and international economic interests and policies. Council programs also fulfill the educational goals of the Atlantic Council by working for an understanding of America's international role by the generations that will succeed to leadership in the next century.

Positions on China and Taiwan

As an institution, the Atlantic Council has no political position on China or Taiwan.

Comment

The Atlantic Council's publications and forums tend to support a carefully balanced U.S. policy toward China that continues MFN treatment for China, a vigorous U.S. engagement with Taiwan that nonetheless avoids serious upset in overall U.S.-China relations, and detailed analysis of the important military and security implications of China's rising power.

The Brookings Institution

Founded: 1916
Focus on China: Included under the Foreign Policy Studies Program.
Membership/Area of Influence: Brookings focuses on governmental studies, foreign policy studies, economic studies, and public policy education.
Activities: Educational, public policy research.
Funding: Individuals, corporations, foundations.
Annual Budget: $18.2 million (1994).
Phone: (202) 797-6000 *Fax:* (202) 797-6004

Primary Goals

The Brookings Institution is a private, nonprofit organization devoted to research, education, and publication in economics, government, foreign policy, and the social sciences generally. Its principal purpose is to bring knowledge to bear on the current and emerging public policy problems facing the American people. In its research, Brookings functions as an independent analyst and critic, committed to publishing its findings for the information of the public. In its conferences and other activities, it serves as a bridge between scholarship and public policy, bringing new knowledge to the attention of decision-makers and affording scholars better insight into public policy issues. Its activities are carried out through its research programs, a publications program, and a Social Science Computation Center.

Positions on China and Taiwan

As a nonpartisan research institution, Brookings has no political position on China or Taiwan.

Comment

Brookings' recent leading scholars on China (Harry Harding, Nicholas Lardy) have been closely identified with views favoring continued MFN treatment for China and avoiding upgrading U.S. ties with Taiwan in ways that would jeopardize U.S.-China relations. It is considered moderate-liberal.

The Cato Institute

Founded: 1977
Focus on China: As part of studies dealing with the U.S. foreign policy program.
Membership/Area of Influence: Public policy research, conferences, lectures.
Activities: Educational, public policy research.
Funding: Individuals, corporations, private foundations.
Annual Budget: $3.8 million (1994).
Phone: (202) 546-0200 *Fax:* (202) 546-0728

Primary Goals and Activities

The Cato Institute is a public policy research foundation dedicated to broadening the parameters of policy debate to allow consideration of more options that are consistent with the traditional American principles of limited government, individual liberty, and peace. To that end, the Cato Institute strives to achieve greater involvement of the intelligent, concerned public in questions of public policy and the proper role of government. To counter the trend of growing government, the Cato Institute undertakes an extensive publications program that addresses the complete spectrum of policy issues. The institute's research covers the full spectrum of U.S. public policy issues: economic policy, civil liberties, environment, and foreign policy. The Cato Institute holds several policy conferences each year, including conferences on monetary issues and on regulatory issues. It also holds briefer Policy Forums each month.

Positions on China and Taiwan

Cato has declared no political position on China or Taiwan.

Comment

The Cato Institute has exerted considerably more influence in Washington in recent years, but its work on China and Taiwan has not been of central importance in the ongoing China policy debate. It is considered conservative.

Carnegie Council on Ethics and International Affairs

Founded: 1914
Focus on China: The Carnegie Council addresses topics of international concern, including China.
Membership/Area of Influence: Through its many publications and sponsored events, the activities of the Carnegie Council reach an international audience.
Activities: Educational.
Funding: The Carnegie Council is funded through investment income, trustees and individual contributions, development program and corporate contributions, and membership fees.
Budget: $1.9 million.
Phone: (212) 838-4120 *Fax:* (212) 752-2432

Primary Goals

The Asia Program, which is the only geographically specific area of study at the Carnegie Council on Ethics and International Affairs, "focuses on the immediate practical policy relevance of the examination of ethics and international affairs. The program considers current issues as faced by American and Asian decisionmakers, and seeks to understand the bases for the decisions made. The Asia Program explores the cultural, philosophical and ethical foundations of American and Asian views of each other." Main areas of interest for the council include human rights and the environment in China and East and Southeast Asia.

Positions on China and Taiwan

The Carnegie Council does not have a defined political position on China and Taiwan.

Comment

Its programs have been notable in considering the option of Taiwan's entry into the United Nations and other world bodies, despite the opposition of mainland China.

Activities

The activities of the Asia Program include hosting panels addressing topics ranging from APEC's influence in the Asia-Pacific region to Taiwan's United Nations membership bid. The program is also interested in democracy and political participation issues. As a major power in Asia, China serves as a focus for much of the council's attention. Recent trends in economic growth have been closely examined, as have human rights. Beginning in 1993 the council started a multi-year program addressing human rights, concentrating on several countries, of which China is one. Entitled "The Growth of East Asia and Its Impact on Human Rights," the program has brought together leaders from government and academia to discuss and present papers on the issue. The first workshop of the series was held in Hakone, Japan, in June 1995. The second meeting took place in Bangkok, Thailand, in March 1996, and a third meeting was held in New York in October 1996.

A second main project for the Asia Program is the project on China's environment. The program, entitled "Cultural Constructions of Social Welfare: A Comparative Study of Environment and Development Values in China, India, Japan, and the U.S.," has the mission of understanding the "normative assumptions that define policy options and conceptions of governance and welfare with respect to shared environmental concerns in four environmentally significant states: China, India, Japan, and the United States." To accomplish this mission, study teams in each country will analyze the factors that influence the views of political players (including economic, political, social, and cultural factors), note the criteria each system uses to assess its goals, and finally make recommendations for improving the welfare assessments in each country.

The Asia Program also devotes a large part of its agenda to addressing political topics in the Greater China area, such as China-Taiwan relations. Some of the more recent projects include studying the relationship between the China and Taiwan and the policy choices available to them, and a conference on "Policy Development in Democracy: U.S.-ROC Relations Toward the 21st Century." The council also sponsored a seminar featuring opposition parties in Taiwan. The Asia Program also hosts a United States-Taiwan Policy Consultation Group.

The Asia Program also sponsors a number of publications or research projects on China.

The Carnegie Endowment for International Peace

Founded: 1910

Focus on China: One of a range of international topics of concern to the institution.
Membership/Area of Influence: The Carnegie Endowment promotes public policy research through publications, conferences, and other meetings.
Activities: Educational, public policy research.
Funding: Endowments, foundations, grants.
Phone: (202) 862-7900

Primary Goals

The Carnegie Endowment for International Peace conducts research, publishing, and training programs pertinent to issues of American foreign policy and diplomacy; humanitarian crises; and international law, security, and peace. The foundation focuses on foreign policy and international issues ranging from European security and East-West issues, to America's national security, to religion and militancy in developing regions of the world.

Positions on China and Taiwan

As a nonprofit, research organization, the Carnegie Endowment has no political position on China or Taiwan.

Comment

Under the recent directorship of Ambassador Morton Abramowitz, the organization showed strong interest in U.S. Asia policy. Its forums and publications tended to argue for a balanced policy toward China, continued MFN treatment for China, and avoiding U.S. initiatives toward Taiwan that would seriously upset U.S.-China relations.

Center for National Security Policy

Founded: 1988
Focus on China: Among other U.S. national security issues.
Purpose and Scope: The Center for National Security Policy is a nonprofit, nonpartisan organization committed to stimulating and informing the national and international debates about all aspects of security policy—notably those policies bearing on the foreign, defense, economic, financial, and technology interests of the United States. It contributes to the debate by the rapid preparation and dissemination of analyses and policy recommendations via computerized facsimile, its World Wide Web site, published articles, and electronic media. The principal audience for such

materials is the U.S. security policymaking community (the executive and legislative branches, the armed forces, and appropriate independent agencies), corresponding organizations in key foreign governments, the press (domestic and international), the global business and financial community, and interested individuals in the public at large.
Phone: (202) 466-0515

Positions on China and Taiwan

Tends to be critical of China and supportive of Taiwan.

Comment

Bulletins and other information from the center tend to be critical of the Chinese government's policies, especially its security policies; strongly supportive of a much tougher U.S. policy toward China than that followed by the Bush and Clinton administrations; and strongly supportive of U.S. ties with Taiwan.

Center for Strategic and International Studies (CSIS)

Founded: 1962
Focus on China: CSIS exists to advance understanding on a wide range of international topics, including China.
Membership/Area of Influence: CSIS is a policy research institute, with a staff of eighty full-time policy analysts, eighty full-time support staff, and sixty-seventy interns.
Activities: Policy research.
Funding: Eighty-five percent of CSIS's funding is donations and grants from individuals and corporations. The balance is obtained through government contracts, publication sales, interest, and conference fees. CSIS maintains strict independence from its sources and will not receive aid from parties who seek to alter the nature and independence of CSIS's research.
Annual Budget: $15 million.
Phone: (202) 887-0200 *Fax:* (202) 775-3199

Primary Goals

The Center for Strategic and International Studies is a public policy research institute, with the goal of advancing understanding of international issues ranging from international economics and business to politics and security. CSIS is nonpartisan in its approach, providing information for the leaders of the country with timely, relevant information. To succeed in its mission, CSIS employs full-time policy analysts to research and publish findings on the various issues that encompass its mission. In the area of Sino-American relations, CSIS studies a wide range of topics varying from economics to strategic military interests. The methodology of CSIS emphasizes a comprehensive research plan, concentrating on areas such as strategic and contingency planning, synergy, and critical policy issues.

Positions on China and Taiwan

CSIS is nonpartisan in its research and thus has no official position on China or Taiwan.

Comment

Recent CSIS forums and publications have emphasized a balanced, constructive U.S. relationship with China; continued MFN treatment for China; a moderate U.S. stance in relation to Hong Kong issues; and avoiding U.S. ties with Taiwan that would seriously disrupt U.S.-mainland China relations.

Highlights of China-Related Efforts: CSIS U.S.-China Policy Task Force. Members of the task force, representing government, business, and academia, monitor issues in China, Taiwan, and Hong Kong. Topics of interest include political and economic trends, proliferation, human rights, and trade.

CSIS Monograph Series on East Asia's Economic and Financial Outlook: Recent monographs have been commissioned to address East Asia's economic future from three different views, representing China, Taiwan, and Hong Kong.

Taipei Roundtable: CSIS experts meet in Taipei with Taiwanese business, government, and academic leaders to discuss issues relating to U.S.-China relations, U.S. policy on Asia, developments in the PRC, and Taiwan's UN membership bid.

CSIS also places emphasis on publication, with numerous works coming from scholars in residence, in addition to the publications produced by CSIS itself.

Center for Taiwan International Relations (CTIR)

Founded: 1988
Focus on China: Entire existence.
Membership/Area of Influence: Offices in Washington, D.C., and New York

City.
Activities: Educational, political.
Funding: Supported by private donations.
Annual Budget: NA.
Phone: (202) 543-6287 *Fax:* (202) 543-2364

Primary Goals

"CTIR has always maintained that the sovereignty of Taiwan (including the Pescadores) belongs to 21 million people of Taiwan, and to no one else. Thus, it supports the right of those people to decide the ultimate resolution of the Taiwan Question. No government constituted without the consent of Taiwan's people has any valid claim to sovereignty over the island or any right to characterize Taiwan's future as its 'internal affairs.' To this end, CTIR works with the international community to uphold the right of Taiwan's people to decide their future for themselves and to ensure that this decision is made freely without threat, coercion, or false information."

Position on China

CTIR asserts that Taiwan is independent of China, and thus China does not have the claim to exercise control over Taiwan or consider Taiwan to be its internal affair.

Position on Taiwan

As long as Taiwan's government is not freely elected, without the fear of oppression or blacklisting, and there is not equal access to the media, CTIR maintains, the people of Taiwan should not feel the Taiwan government has any valid claim or representation.

Activities

CTIR is engaged in research activities, conducting policy analysis on issues concerning Taiwan. Additionally, CTIR works to develop contacts with government officials around the world to generate support for the independence movement in Taiwan. CTIR is working to establish dialogue with policymakers and to "facilitate contacts between government, social, human rights, environmental, and culture organizations in Taiwan and their counterparts worldwide."

In order to create these relationships, CTIR provides speakers for seminars on Taiwan issues and has provided expert testimony in Congress.

CTIR disseminates information on Taiwan, gives editorials to newspapers, and seeks to use the media to carry its message to the American public.

In recent years, the Center for Taiwan International Relations has hosted conferences in the United States on a wide range of Taiwanese topics.

Comment

The Center for Taiwan International Relations contributes importantly to the work of the range of groups in the United States supporting Taiwan's greater role in world affairs.

China Information and Culture Center

Focus on China: Entire existence, but centered on the Republic of China on Taiwan.
Membership/Area of Influence: The center is located in New York, but with wider influence.
Activities: Educational, cultural.
Funding: The center is funded by the government of Taiwan and private donations.
Annual Budget: NA.
Phone: (212) 373-1800 *Fax:* (212) 373-1867

Primary Goals

The China Information and Culture Center is the largest public resource center in the New York area focusing on Chinese culture and contemporary life on Taiwan. Encompassing a theater, an art gallery, a library, and a culture center, the CICC serves to promote, educate, and inform researchers and the general public on Chinese issues. Books, videos, films, and documents may be lent, and the center sponsors many cultural programs on the premises.

Positions on China and Taiwan

CICC is funded and supported by the government of Taiwan; the materials located in the center have their origins and focus in Taiwan. Periodicals and multimedia resources reflect various positions on the state of events in Taiwan and China.

Comment

CICC is another concrete example of how the Taiwan government sees its interests as well served by spending money in order to reach out to a broad range of the U.S. public and to familiarize it with the developments and aspirations of the people of Taiwan.

Activities

CICC's various components sponsor a number of events and activities. The Taipei Theater presents puppetry, Chinese opera, Chinese music, and various other artistic groups from Taiwan. Past performers have included the National Experimental Chinese Orchestra, the Lan-Yang Taiwanese Opera Troupe, the Taipei Philharmonic Chorus, Hsiao Hsi Yuan Puppet Theater, Hsiao Hsi Yuan Puppet Theater Master Class, and the Wang Hai-Ling with the Flying Horse Opera Troupe. Performers have demonstrated both modern and traditional arts.

The Taipei Gallery exhibits both ancient and contemporary Chinese art from Taiwan. The pieces are on loan from private collectors and museums in Taiwan. The gallery also displays international art that relates to Chinese themes.

To reach a greater audience, CICC sponsors television programs in the New York area with the purpose of introducing Chinese culture. In addition, the center offers cultural classes to the public with the range of subjects including Mandarin Chinese, Calligraphy, Chinese Martial Arts, Chinese Ink Painting, Chinese Decorative Knotting, and Paper Folding.

With over 30,000 volumes in both English and Chinese, the CICC library collection's main focus is on culture and life in Taiwan. Special collections include juvenile literature, classical Chinese literature, Buddhist doctrine, East Asian history, Chinese philosophy, and Chinese modern arts. CICC also has a "comprehensive collection on the history of post-1945 Taiwan." CICC has a special collection of government publications from Taiwan,"the most complete record of its kind in the U.S."

Committee of 100 for Tibet

Founded: 1992
Focus on China: The committee has focused on Tibet, which is currently "occupied" by China, since its inception.
Membership/Area of Influence: The committee, as its name implies, has 100 members from around the world.
Activities: Educational, political.

Funding: NA.
Annual Budget: NA.

Primary Goals

The role of the Committee of 100 for Tibet is to inform the public about the unique national, cultural, and religious identity of the Tibetan people and to work to preserve that identity and ensure the survival and human rights of the Tibetan people. The committee is dedicated to placing Tibet on the international agenda, and to encouraging peoples and governments to recognize that Tibet is currently illegally occupied and colonized by China.

Activities

The Committee of 100 for Tibet actively works with other Tibet support organizations to promote ideas and news about Tibet. Through the World Tibet Network News (WTN), and the *Tibet News Digest,* the committee hopes to garner world support for a free and independent Tibet.

Comment

The committee's impact on policy is hard to measure, though its role appears secondary to such organizations as the International Campaign for Tibet (see following).

Council on Foreign Relations

Founded: 1921
Focus on China: The Council on Foreign Relations addresses issues in foreign relations, including China.
Membership/Area of Influence: The council has approximately 3,000 members, representing all areas of business, government, academia, media, and society in general. Members must be citizens of the United States or permanent residents who have applied for citizenship.
Activities: Educational.
Funding: The council is funded through a combination of membership dues, both corporate and private, donations, grants, book publications, investments, fellowships, and publication of *Foreign Affairs* magazine.
Annual Budget: $15.5 million.
Phone: (212)734-0400 *Fax:* (212)861-1789

Primary Goals

"The Council on Foreign Relations was founded in 1921, and is dedicated to the continuous study of U.S. foreign policy for the benefit of both its members and a wider American and world audience. The Council serves as a center for scholarship and policy analysis, as a membership organization, and as a public education organization, reaching out nationally and internationally to disseminate ideas and collaborate with other institutions."

Positions on China and Taiwan

"The Council takes no institutional position on issues of foreign policy; it is host to many views, advocate of none. No one is authorized to speak on behalf of the council on any matter of public policy."

Comment

Council forums and publications have tended to support a carefully balanced approach to China and continued MFN treatment. The council showed recent interest in Taiwan and U.S.-Taiwan relations; its forums and publications tend to eschew policies that would seriously disrupt U.S.-mainland China relations.

Activities

The Council on Foreign Relations is involved in a number of activities relevant to China including Study Programs, Meetings Programs, Corporate Programs, Washington Programs, National Programs, and International Affairs Fellowships.

A Studies Program "organizes study groups and update meetings and produces publications that examine in depth major issues of concern to U.S. policymakers. Studies strive to identify U.S. national interests, analyze the factors that will affect them, and propose a wide range of realistic American policy options to address them."

East-West Center

Founded: 1960
Focus on China: Entire existence.
Membership/Area of Influence: The East-West Center is located in Hawaii, with a staff of 295, including fifty-five research positions, but its influence

stretches through the Pacific Rim.

Resources: 44,000 books, 22,000 periodicals, special collections include resource material collection, culture, communications, Pacific islands, population, environment policy, and minerals.

Funding: Funds allocated by the U.S. Congress, donations from foreign governments, donations from private corporations, and contract research (less than 25 percent of revenue).

Annual Budget: $26 million (1994).

Phone: (808) 944-7111 *Fax:* (808) 944-7970

Primary Goals

"The East-West Center aims to promote better relations and understanding among the nations of Asia, the Pacific, and the United States through cooperative study, training, and research." Established in 1960 by the U.S. Congress, and part of the University of Hawaii until 1975, the Center is currently an independent nonpartisan institution."

The purpose of the East-West Center is to provide a neutral site where leaders in academia, government, and business from around the world can meet and work with the center staff to address "issues of contemporary significance in such areas as international economics and politics, the environment, population, energy and mineral resources, cultural studies, communications, the media, and Pacific islands development."

Positions on China and Taiwan

The center carefully avoids taking positions on such issues in U.S. policy.

Comment

Scholars at the center, including the recent president, Michel Oksenberg, have tended to support a constructive U.S. relationship with China, continued MFN treatment, and a low-key U.S. posture in relations with Taiwan.

Emergency Committee for American Trade (ECAT)

Founded: 1967

Focus on China: Recent years.

Membership/Area of Influence: ECAT's members account for major segments of the manufacturing, banking, processing, merchandising, and publishing

sectors of the American economy. Their worldwide sales in 1992 totaled over $1 trillion and they have over 5 million employees.
Activities: Educational, political.
Funding: NA.
Phone: (202) 659-5147 *Fax:* (202) 659-1347

Primary Goals

ECAT's purpose is to support measures that facilitate an expanding international economic system.

Positions on China and Taiwan

Strongly favors continuation of MFN tariff treatment for China. The long-term goal is to move beyond the ad hoc, conditional arrangements of the cold war trade statutes, such as Jackson-Vanik, to a new structure that includes: (1) China's accession to the World Trade Organization (WTO), based on a commercially acceptable protocol and the U.S. extension of permanent MFN treatment; (2) lifting eligibility restrictions for Overseas Private Investment Corporation (OPIC) insurance and Trade and Development Agency (TDA) assistance, which have been ineffective and have only hurt U.S. companies; and (3) revising restrictive U.S. trade regulations that target China. All these elements are premised on China's willingness to accept its responsibilities within the international community.

Activities

Members of ECAT, supported by experts from within their companies and from the small ECAT staff, have made their views known through testimony before congressional committees, through contacts with congressional and administration officials, through liaison with other organizations, and through public information programs.

Over the last several years, ECAT has chaired the Business Coalition for U.S.-China Trade, which consists of ECAT member companies as well as other U.S. companies, trade associations, farm organizations, and consumer groups. The group was formed to coordinate business support for the continuation of MFN treatment to China and the expansion of trade and investment in China.

ECAT has worked with the coalition to develop a step-by-step approach, involving reciprocal actions by the United States and China, to restructure bilateral trade relations and to eliminate the highly disruptive annual debates over the extension of MFN to China. The strategy is premised on the notion that U.S. trade and engagement have contributed to significant improvements in the economic, political, and social well-being of the Chinese people and offer the greatest promise for further progress in China.

The strategy advocates the adoption of the following five core points as governing principles in the conduct of U.S.-China commercial relations:

- MFN must continue;
- The United States should stick to its policy of comprehensive engagement;
- The solution to trade imbalances is to expand American exports, not to close American markets;
- Trade and engagement promote long-term progress on human rights; and
- The United States should not abandon its "One China" policy.

Comment

ECAT is central to the "business lobby" on China in Washington. Its large influence is an essential reason business interests have prevailed in the ongoing tug-of-war in Washington over MFN for China.

The Family Research Council (FRC)

Founded: 1983
Focus on China: Recent years.
Activities: Educational, political.
Funding: FRC is a nonpartisan, nonprofit organization, recognized under Section 501(a) of the Internal Revenue Code as tax-exempt.
Annual Budget: NA.
Phone: (202) 393-2100 *Fax:* (202) 393-2134

Primary Goals

"The Family Research Council's primary reason for existence is to reaffirm and promote nationally and particularly in Washington, D.C., the traditional family and the Judeo-Christian principles upon which it is built."

Position on China

FRC is nonpartisan.

Comment

Recent FRC publications have strongly criticized Chinese government human rights practices, especially regarding coercive abortion, and its persecution of Christians and other religious believers. FRC strongly urges revocation of U.S. MFN trade privileges to China on account of China's continued human rights abuses. In 1997, FRC beefed up its efforts on China policy, becoming perhaps the leading force in the effort to halt MFN treatment for China.

Activities

Newsletters, ad hoc publications, and testimony before congressional committees.

Formosan Association for Public Affairs (FAPA)

Founded: 1982
Focus on China: Entire existence.
Membership/Area of Influence: Twenty-four chapters in North America. Total membership in the United States is around 1,000 families.
Activities: Educational, political.
Funding: Accomplished solely through private donations from Taiwanese-American families.
Annual Budget: Approximately $120,000.
Phone: (202) 786-1615 *Fax:* (202) 543-7891

Primary Goals

To seek international support for the right of the people of Taiwan (Formosa) to determine their future status; to promote human rights, freedom, and democracy for the people of Taiwan; to protect and enhance the rights, interests, and welfare of Taiwanese communities throughout the world.

Position on China

FAPA favors the development and continuing of friendly relations between the United States and China. However, China should not be allowed to force its views on Taiwan as a province of China on other nations as a condition of establishing friendly relations. China has no jurisdiction over Taiwan, demonstrated by the 1952 San Francisco Peace Treaty, which left Taiwan's international status open and ambiguous. To that end, China needs to renounce all claims of jurisdiction over Taiwan or the threat of using military force to subjugate the island.

Position on Taiwan

FAPA believes that the Taiwanese government, although moving slowly in the direction of democracy and freedom, needs to move faster toward holding universal free and open elections, finally allowing the people of Taiwan to choose their own government, including opposition parties. The traditionally Kuomintang (KMT)-controlled government needs to allow open elections without fear of political or police repression.

FAPA sees the United States as the most important external factor with the ability to influence policymaking on Taiwan and on improving Taiwan's international status through UN membership or complete separation from China. FAPA hopes the United States will use its position in international affairs to persuade a number of influential nations who would support Taiwan's independence in the face of Chinese opposition.

Comment

FAPA is the leading Taiwanese-American organization dealing with U.S.-China policy and Taiwan. It has some following on Capitol Hill, and makes its views widely heard, despite its relatively small budget. It plays an important role in getting Congress to consider and pass legislation that advocates greater U.S. support for Taiwan and the people of Taiwan.

The Heritage Foundation

Founded: 1973

Focus on China: Since 1983 the Heritage Foundation has had an Asian Studies Center, of which the study of China is a part.

Membership/Area of Influence: The Heritage Foundation's works and publications reach across the country.

Activities: Educational.

Funding: Funding is accomplished through a combination of individual and corporate donations, investment income, foundation grants, and publication sales.

Annual Budget: Approximately $22 million.

Phone: (202) 546-4400

Primary Goals

"The Heritage Foundation is a research and educational institute—a think tank—whose mission is to formulate and promote conservative public policies based on the principles of free enterprise, limited government, individual freedom, traditional American values, and a strong national defense."

Positions on China and Taiwan

The Heritage Foundation is a nonpartisan, public policy research institute. As such it has no official position toward China or Taiwan.

Comment

Heritage is the most active of conservative think tanks dealing with China policy. It has a strong record of urging firm U.S. support for Taiwan; this is balanced by its strong support for continued MFN treatment for China. Indeed, Heritage was among the first in the United States to argue for continued MFN treatment and continued constructive U.S. relations with Beijing in the period immediately after the 1989 Tiananmen incident.

Activities

Started in 1983, the Asian Studies Center of the Heritage Foundation has worked on creating effective public policy to address the issues the United States faces in the Asia-Pacific region. The Asian Studies Center regularly sponsors conferences on a variety of Asian topics, inviting leading scholars and political figures to participate. The Heritage Foundation also publishes a number of policy papers each year.

Hoover Institution (Stanford University)

Founded: 1919
Focus on China: Began in 1945.
Membership/Area of Influence: The Hoover Institution, as part of Stanford University, has a wide area of influence, coupling scholarship with publication. The institution has a staff of 280, of which eighty are in research positions.
Activities: Educational.
Annual Budget: $19 million.
Phone: (415) 723-0603 *Fax:* (415) 723-1687

Primary Goals

The Hoover Institution in general is devoted to research in the social sciences and public policy concerning domestic and international affairs. With regard to the Asian Research Program, "emphasis is naturally upon relations between the United States and Asia in the twentieth century. Within this frame of reference, much attention is given to the internal affairs of Asian nations, particularly China and Japan, and to their relations with each other."

Positions on China and Taiwan

The Hoover Institution is a nonpartisan research institution and has no specific position on China or Taiwan.

Comment

Hoover Institution forums and publications have in the recent past been identified with a strong support for Taiwan and a somewhat critical view of mainland China. More recent events and publications support a constructive U.S. policy toward China and a moderate U.S. stance toward Taiwan that will not seriously upset U.S.-China relations.

Activities

As a research institution, Hoover's activities revolve around research and publication.

Human Rights in China

Founded: 1989
Focus on China: Entire existence.
Activities: Educational (human rights), political.
Funding: HRIC is a nonprofit organization, which depends solely on private, tax-deductible donations. It does not accept funding with any political conditions.
Annual Budget: NA.
Phone: (212) 661-2909 *Fax:* (212) 972-0905

Primary Goals

Founded by Chinese scientists and scholars, Human Rights in China

Primary Goals

The International Campaign for Tibet's primary goal is helping to obtain independence for the people of Tibet, who, the ICT says, are held in a colonial state by the People's Republic of China. In reaching for this goal, ICT is hoping through its efforts around the world to create support for Tibet and to force China to begin serious, substantive talks on Tibet's occupation.

Position on China

ICT views the Chinese as illegally seizing and controlling their homeland. The Chinese militarily conquered Tibet in 1949, and their claims that Tibet is a traditional part of China have no basis, according to Tibetan supporters. ICT, opposing this Chinese oppression, is pressing the leaders of the PRC to remove its presence from the mountain nation.

Comment

International Campaign for Tibet is the most influential Tibetan advocacy group in the recent U.S. policy debate. It keeps its focus on Tibet-related questions and tends to avoid direct involvement in other aspects of the U.S.-China policy debate.

International Republican Institute (IRI)

Founded: IRI, 1984; China Program, 1993.
Focus on China: Since 1993.
Membership/Area of Influence: The International Republican Institute conducts programs in thirty-four countries and has offices in ten. There is no office in China. The Washington, D.C., office has a staff of approximately sixty-five persons, with an additional staff of thirteen working outside the United States. Additionally, IRI uses hundreds of volunteers to staff the overseas missions.
Activities: Political, educational.
Funding: For 1995, approximately $3.3 million from the National Endowment for Democracy, $7 million in grants from the Agency for International Development, $800,000 from the African Regional Electoral Assistance Fund, and $200,000 in private donations from individuals and corporations.
Annual Budget: For China, approximately $430,000.
Phone: (202) 408-9450 *Fax:* (202) 408-9462

Primary Goals (Regarding China)

- Strengthen the voice of Chinese calling for political and economic change by assisting on independent public policy formulation, legislative reform, and electoral initiatives.
- IRI works with the Institute for Global Concern, a native voluntary organization, to further attempts for independent legislative action through creating studies examining legislative initiatives in banking and real estate reform. IRI also seeks to work with the National People's Congress, researching issues that arise through the assembly.
- Reform Chinese legislatures and central-provincial legislative relations through cooperative work with the Institute of Legal Culture. Additionally, work to complete proposals for legislative reform.
- Strengthen ability of local institutions to conduct legitimate, competitive elections.

Position on China

IRI has no specific position on China or on Sino-American relations and is currently involved in assisting the Chinese government in drafting and revising legislative and economic reform. IRI also has no position on the Chinese Communist Party and its role in the governing of the PRC.

Comment

IRI's innovative programs in and with China would be in jeopardy if U.S.-China relations were to become hostile after such an action as U.S. withdrawal of MFN treatment or a U.S.-PRC confrontation over Taiwan.

Kettering Foundation

Founded: 1927
Interest in China: Recent years.
Purpose and Scope: The Kettering Foundation is a nonprofit, operating foundation that does not make grants but welcomes partnerships with other institutions (or groups of institutions) and individuals who are actively working on problems of communities, politics, and education.

Comment

The Kettering Foundation was notable as one of the first U.S. groups to actively promote contacts with Chinese government-affiliated institutions in the aftermath of the 1989 Tiananmen incident.

Mansfield Center for Pacific Affairs

The Mansfield Center is the public policy and international outreach arm of the Maureen and Mike Mansfield Foundation. Established in 1983, the foundation was created to build on Ambassador Mansfield's lifelong efforts to bring about a better understanding between the United States and Asia. The center maintains offices in Washington, D.C.; Missoula, Montana; and Tokyo.

Activities

Focusing on policymakers and opinion leaders—especially young, emerging leaders—the center promotes and nurtures enduring relationships. Working through lectures, forums, seminars, conferences, and publications, the center provides avenues for in-depth exploration of evolving issues. Examples of the work currently being undertaken by the center include administering the Mansfield Fellowship Program, created to send U.S. government officials to Japan for one year of work in Japanese government ministries, preceded by a year of full-time Japanese-language training; organizing a forum in Tokyo for discussion of perspective and policies on the China-Taiwan-Hong Kong triangular relationships; presenting a telecommunications symposium in Tokyo that will examine the steps toward implementation being undertaken by the signatories to the World Trade Organization agreement on telecommunications; and sponsoring a major research project comparing journalistic values in the United States and Japan.

Comment

In recent years, the Mansfield Center has become more involved in China-related issues in Washington in ways that associate it with those arguing for a constructive relationship with China. Thus, it has sponsored a dinner designed to showcase leading PRC luminaries speaking on Hong Kong issues, and it has sponsored visits to China by congressional staff.

Market Access Ltd.

Comment

This company, located in Hong Kong, is the home base of John Kamm. A former president of the U.S. Chamber of Commerce in Hong

Kong, Kamm has worked with more effectiveness than other human rights advocates in gaining the release of prisoners of conscience in China. Against this background, he has been called on repeatedly by U.S. executive and legislative officials for advice on how to deal with China, especially over human rights questions.

Kamm generally favors a firm stance on human rights questions, though he also tends to favor continued MFN treatment for China, albeit with some conditions. He is not active on Taiwan-related issues.

National Bureau of Asian Research (NBR)

Founded: 1989
Focus on China: NBR addresses a number of Asian topics, including but not limited to China.
Membership/Area of Influence: NBR serves as an international clearinghouse of information on Asian issues.
Activities: Educational.
Funding: NBR's funding is provided through foundations, government grants, and private donations.
Annual Budget: NA.
Phone: (206) 632-7370 *Fax:* (206) 632-7487

Primary Goals

The function of the National Bureau of Asian Research is to serve as a nonpartisan, international clearinghouse on policy issues relating to the Asian Pacific.

Positions on China and Taiwan

The National Bureau of Asian Research is nonpartisan in its approach and has no political position on China or Taiwan.

Comment

NBR's research and seminars tend to emphasize a pragmatic and constructive U.S. policy toward China, continued MFN treatment for China, and a moderate U.S. stance toward Taiwan that would not jeopardize U.S.-mainland China relations.

Activities

The activity for which NBR is most noted is its ability to draw upon specialists from around the world on a variety of topics. NBR tracks over 2,000 specialists, and uses their expertise to address the issue at hand. NBR sponsors research on a variety of China-related issues.

National Committee for United States-China Relations

Focus on China: Entire existence.
Membership/Area of Influence: The National Committee has 650 members, all of whom are distinguished Americans who share an interest and belief that U.S.-China relations can be strengthened through public knowledge and education. The committee has a sixty-three-member board with one chairperson and six vice chairs.
Activities: Educational/exchange/policy development.
Funding: The National Committee is funded through a combination of grants from the U.S. Information Agency, U.S. Department of Education, foundations, and private donations.
Annual Budget: NA.
Phone: (212) 922-1385 *Fax:* (212) 645-1695

Primary Goals and Activities

The National Committee for U.S.-China Relations is a nonprofit organization that believes U.S.-China relations can be strengthened through greater public education. The committee focuses on personnel exchange, education, and policy activities in areas such as economic development, governance and legal affairs, international relations, education administration, and environmental issues. To best achieve these aims the National Committee is divided into six program areas: governance and legal affairs, economic development and management, education administration, international affairs, mass communication, and environmental and global affairs.

Positions on China and Taiwan

The National Committee is nonpartisan.

Comment

National Committee officers, headed by President David Michael Lampton, are in the lead in urging the United States to adopt constructive policies toward China. They favor continued MFN treatment for China and a moderate U.S. stance toward Taiwan that would avoid seriously jeopardizing U.S. relations with mainland China.

The Nonproliferation Policy Education Center (NPEC)

Founded: 1994
Focus on China: As it relates to the proliferation of weapons of mass destruction.
Membership/Area of Influence: Works to educate policymakers, journalists, and university professors.
Funding: NA.
Phone: (202) 466-4406 *Fax:* (202) 659-5429

Primary Goals and Activities

NPEC educates policymakers, journalists, and university professors about proliferation threats and possible new policies and measures to meet them. NPEC's key aims include:

- Filling critical gaps in the literature concerning key perspectives on proliferation and nonproliferation policy. NPEC commissions policy-oriented monographs addressing key issues and challenges to U.S. and international security.
- Promoting a deeper understanding of the relevance of these perspectives on proliferation. NPEC brings together congressional staff, administration officials, and the press to discuss pressing proliferation issues at a series of seminars.
- Institutionalizing teaching about proliferation issues. NPEC makes teaching materials available to college and graduate school professors and conducts seminars for key national security professors around the country.

Position on China

NPEC is nonpartisan.

Comment

Congressional testimony by NPEC Executive Director Henry Sokolski has been critical of China's weapons development and proliferation policies.

Pacific Basin Economic Council (PBEC)

Founded: 1967
Focus on China: Pacific Basin, including China.
Membership/Area of Influence: The membership of PBEC includes more that 1,100 corporate members in nineteen economies and countries, including China, Chinese Taipei, Hong Kong, and the United States.
Activities: Economic.
Funding: Supported by members.
Annual Budget: NA.
Phone: (808) 521-9044 *Fax:* (808) 521-8530

Primary Goals

The mission of the PBEC is to "achieve a business environment in the region that ensures open trade and investment and encourages competitiveness based on the capabilities of individual companies. It provides information, networking fora, and services to members that increase their business opportunities."

Positions on China and Taiwan

As an organization dedicated to economic pursuits, PBEC has no political position. PBEC members consist of both countries and economies; both China and Taiwan participate in PBEC.

Activities

PBEC hosts the Annual International General Meeting, "which brings together more than 700 business leaders, government ministers, and heads of state to discuss emerging business opportunities and trade issues facing the region."

PBEC serves also as a liaison between business leaders and government officials. PBEC provides advice on development issues in the Pacific region. It also conducts business symposiums, whose focus is on improving the business climate in the region, "effectively working with the business community toward the common goals of trade and investment liberalization, and increasing economic growth and prosperity."

Comment

By focusing on economic issues, PBEC avoids many of the complications in U.S.-PRC-Taiwan relations. Its forums and members tend to be strongly supportive of a constructive U.S. relationship with China, including continued MFN treatment for China.

Pacific Economic Cooperation Council (PECC)

Founded: 1980; U.S. National Committee, 1984.
Focus on China: The goals of the group focus on improving economic relations in the Pacific Rim region, including China.
Membership/Area of Influence: The organization includes 22 Asia-Pacific "economies," with some of the more prominent members, including China, Japan, Korea, Hong Kong, Chinese Taipei (Taiwan), Russia, and the United States. The international secretariat is based in Singapore. The U.S. committee is composed of leaders in government, business, and institutions. Its headquarters are located in Washington, D.C.
Activities: Economic.
Funding: Provided by the member economies. The U.S. Committee is supported by private and government grants, as well as business contributions.
Annual Budget: NA.
Phone: U.S. (202) 745-7444; Singapore (65) 737-9822/3 *Fax:* (65) 737-9824

Primary Goals

The primary objective of the Pacific Economic Cooperation Council is to provide an open informal forum in which member economies can work together to pursue cooperative economic ventures in a neutral environment. The PECC is not a negotiating body.

Position on China

PECC is a nonpartisan group, seeking to provide a nonconfrontational forum where views can be shared and agreements reached to create a more open and economically stable Asia-Pacific area. Both China and Taiwan (referred to as Chinese Taipei), are members of PECC.

Comment

By focusing on economic relations, PECC avoids many issues of controversy in U.S.-PRC-Taiwan relations. Its members tend to favor moderate and constructive U.S. relations with mainland China, including U.S. MFN treatment for China.

Taiwan International Alliance

Founded: September 1991
Focus on China: Entire existence.
Membership/Area of Influence: TIA addresses issues relating to a free Taiwan in both Taiwan and the United States. TIA has two offices; its main one is in Taipei, Taiwan, with another office in New York City.
Activities: Educational, political.
Funding: TIA is a nonprofit organization funded through private donations and contributions from members and supporters. TIA also does its own fund-raising.
Annual Budget: NA.
Phone: New York Office (212) 983-0480 *Fax:* (212) 983-1097

Primary Goals

"The mission of Taiwan International Alliance is to differentiate Taiwan from China, thus overcoming twenty years of international isolation. By educating the world community about the history and accomplishments of Taiwan and its peoples, Taiwan can regain international recognition as a nation state with a seat in the United Nations and all other international forums."

Position on China

The Taiwan International Alliance holds that Taiwan is not part of China and that China has no legitimate claim on the island in view of the San Francisco Treaty at the end of World War II, coupled with the 1895 Treaty of Shimoneski, in which China ceded Taiwan to Japan. At the of World War II, Japan relinquished her colonies, including Taiwan. Because there is no specific reference in the San Francisco Treaty regarding control of the island, it is the TIA's position that there is no legislation that gives control of Taiwan to China; thus Taiwan is and should be recognized as an independent nation. To this end, TIA strongly opposes China's claims on Taiwan and seeks to create a sense of international public opinion that will force China to give up its claims to the island.

Position on Taiwan

Taiwan is an independent island and should be recognized as such. The leadership of the island should be chosen through free and open elections. Taiwan, not a part of China, thus should be addressed not as the

Republic of China, but as Taiwan. TIA supports the idea that the Taiwanese people should be able to decide their leadership, status, and future for themselves.

Comment

This group has been closely identified with Taiwan politician Annette Liu, a prominent member of the opposition Democratic Progressive Party. Ms. Liu has not given as much attention to the Alliance recently as in past years.

USA-ROC Economic Council

Founded: 1976
Focus on China: Entire existence.
Membership/Area of Influence: Approximately 220 members, most representing American business, with the rest coming from individuals or state organizations. The council's headquarters are in Washington, D.C., and it has a staff of four.
Activities: Economic/political.
Funding: Funding comes from membership dues and government grants.
Annual Budget: $650,000.
Phone: (202) 331-8966 *Fax:* (202) 331-8985

Primary Goals

"Our organization exists to promote trade relations between the United States and Taiwan, to ensure that U.S. corporations have the best possible chance of securing contracts and investment opportunities in Taiwan."

Positions on China and Taiwan

"The Council takes no political position on the relationship between the United States and Taiwan, nor the United States and China."

Services

Sponsors trade conferences for U.S. and Taiwanese businesses; sponsors trade missions from Taiwan ranging from agricultural to environmental to telecommunications; arranges meetings with leaders of Taiwanese government, business, and industry; promotes trade and improves contact with members of Congress.

Comment

This is the leading group of the U.S.-Taiwan business "lobby" in the United States. It works effectively to be sure that U.S.-Taiwan economic interests are safeguarded and generally eschews extreme positions that would damage those interests. Its members tend to favor continued MFN treatment for China.

U.S.-Asia Institute

Founded: 1980s
Focus on China: Entire existence.
Purpose and Scope: A small not-for-profit organization based in Washington, D.C., that spends much of its effort facilitating U.S.-China exchanges, especially those involving the U.S. congress.

Comment

Since 1980, the institute has been the most active group in arranging visits by congressional staff delegations to China, usually two or more delegations of around ten staff people, each year.

United States Catholic Conference (USCC)

This is the public policy research, advocacy, and outreach arm of the Catholic Church in the United States.

Comment

The United States Catholic Conference (USCC) was the primary church group active in the 1994 debate on China's MFN status. The USCC took part in the MFN debate due to its concern for the underground Catholic Church in China, particularly persecution of Catholics as well as non-Catholic Christians. Though the USCC did not advocate any specific policy during the MFN debate, it did state generally that China should pay a "serious price. . .for violation of fundamental rights" and that the USCC supported some kind of MFN conditioning for China on its human rights performance.

Actions by the USCC included providing testimony before Congress; issuing a letter on May 17, 1994, to Secretary of State Warren Christopher to express the views of the USCC and draw attention to human rights abuses in China; and encouraging letter writing by its members to Congress. The latter activity was done, according to Thomas Quigley, policy adviser in the Department of Social Development and World Peace of the USCC, by

> the sending of packs of materials—with MFN being one of many social issues—by the USCC to all of the dioceses across America who worked closely with social action directors, the principal communicators with socially active Catholics. The directors would encourage the people to communicate with their congress-men to take into consideration human rights in China when contemplating policy. (Cited in Campbell, Steven J., *Grass Roots Lobbying and Coalition Lobbying*, Thesis, University of Louisville, December 1996, p. 62.)

The involvement of the USCC in the 1994 MFN debate brought great numbers of constituencies to the table, expanding the influence of the anti-MFN renewal lobby. Though the USCC did support some kind of MFN conditioning on China's MFN status, no specific policy was advocated. Thus, the nonspecific policy stance of the USCC hindered greater coordination between the USCC and other lobby members. The USCC remained prominent and adopted similar positions in the MFN debate in Congress in later years.

The United States-China Business Council

Founded: 1973 as the National Council for U.S.-China Trade.
Focus on China: Entire existence.
Membership/Area of Influence: The council's membership is made up of 290 firms, ranging from large corporations to small service firms. The council has its headquarters in Washington, D.C., with an office in Beijing, PRC, and a representative in Hong Kong. The council has a full-time staff of eighteen.
Activities: Political/economic.
Funding: The council is supported by contributions from its members.
Annual Budget: NA.
Phone: (202) 429-0340 *Fax:* (202) 775-2476

Primary Goals

To assist firms entering trade relations with China for the first time; to serve and protect the business interests of American firms already established in China; to protect and expand American international trade policy, including the support of most-favored-nation (MFN) status for China; and promote the idea that economic and commercial relations form the basis of the U.S.-China relationship.

Positions on China and Taiwan

The council is dedicated to economic pursuits and does not hold a political position on United States-China or United States-Taiwan relations. The council feels commercial relations are at the heart of U.S.-China relations and hopes through mutual trade to produce a stable and prosperous relationship.

Services

Sponsors trade conferences for American and Chinese businesses, as well as national conferences for American business on economic issues in China, such as a 1994 conference on China's infrastructure development; arranges meetings with leaders of Chinese government, business, and industry, such as Vice Premier Zou Jiahua, Minister of Foreign Trade Wu Yi, and Patent Office Director Gao Lulin; informs its members through notes and briefings of issues in China related to economics, with their possible impacts on American business (i.e., China's government structure, updates on China's economy, Chinese politics, foreign investment opportunities, including recently opened areas such as accounting, banking, infrastructure, and foreign insurance operations); provides its members with the most recent data and statistics on the state of Sino-American trade; and works to maintain free trade between China and the United States.

"The U.S.-China Business Council takes an active role on U.S. policy issues relating to China and to international trade more broadly. It has for several years worked on the recurrent issue of renewed Most Favored Nation trade status for the People's Republic of China, leading the fight for renewal of such trade status without condition." According to President Robert Kapp, "The U.S.-China Business Council and our allies will be doing our utmost to defend normal economic and trade relations between the two countries." The council argues that MFN status gives no special treatment to China but is merely the norm in all American international economic relations except for a handful of countries.

Comment

The council is the most prominent group in Washington focused exclusively on U.S.-China economic issues. Its officers and publications strongly support a constructive U.S. relationship with China and continuation of the current low-level U.S. relationship with Taiwan. They seek permanent MFN treatment for China.

United States-China Peoples'
Friendship Association (USCPFA)

Founded: 1974
Focus on China: Entire existence.
Membership/Area of Influence: Composed of four regions with members in fifty chapters. A national office in New York and regional offices assist local chapters.
Activities: Educational, with an emphasis on promoting U.S.-China friendship.
Funding: A nonprofit, educational organization.
Phone: (212) 989-5094

Primary Goals

The USCPFA's goal is to build active and lasting friendship based on mutual understanding between the people of the United States and the people of China. It recognizes that friendship between the two peoples must be based on the knowledge of and respect for the sovereignty of each country; therefore, it supports the declaration of the United States of America and the People's Republic of China that the resolution of the status of Taiwan is the internal affair of the Chinese on both sides of the Taiwan Straits. It also recognizes that friendship between the two peoples and good relations between the two governments play a critical role in maintaining peace in the Pacific Basin and in the world.

An educational organization, its activities include sponsoring speakers and programs that inform the American people about China; organizing tours and special study groups to China; publishing newsletters and other literature; promoting friendship with Chinese students and scholars while in the United States; and promoting cultural, commercial, technical, and educational exchanges.

Comment

USCPFA suffered in the wake of the Tiananmen incident, as many Americans became less interested in "friendship" with the Chinese government. It continues to work diligently building better understanding between the two societies. Its officers tend to support continued MFN treatment for China and a U.S. relationship with Taiwan that is not offensive to mainland China.

United States Institute of Peace

Founded: 1984
Focus on China: The institute focuses on a number of regional topics, including China.
Membership/Area of Influence: Through its publications, grants, fellowships, and conferences, the institute is able to influence policymaking around the world.
Activities: Educational.
Funding: The institute is funded by Congress as an independent, nonprofit corporation.
Phone: (202) 457-1700 *Fax:* (202) 429-6063

Primary Goals

The mandate of the United States Institute of Peace is to "apply the lessons learned from history and our national experience to the challenge of achieving peace among nations."

Positions on China and Taiwan

As a nonpartisan, research institute, the institute has no political position on China or Taiwan.

Comment

The institute's leading officers in recent years have included Richard Solomon (president), Alan Romberg, and Stanley Roth. All are closely identified with support for a constructive U.S. policy toward China, continued MFN treatment for China, and a moderate U.S. policy toward Taiwan that would not seriously upset U.S.-mainland China relations.

Washington Center for Chinese Studies

Founded: January 1990
Focus on China: Entire existence.
Membership/Area of Influence: The center extends its influence through a wide range of programs including research, teaching, and fellowship programs, publications, and exchanges of information, and publications. The membership consists primarily of overseas Chinese scholars.
Activities: Educational.
Funding: The center is a "not for profit," independent organization supported

by contributions from foundations, corporations, and individuals.
Phone: (202)-296-8071 *Fax:* (202)-296-8072

Primary Goals

The goals of WCCS are to organize, coordinate, and support Chinese scholars conducting studies on pressing Chinese issues, and to promote active exchange and better understanding between China and the world. The center serves multiple functions as a think tank for China studies, a human resource center, and a gateway to information on China. It conducts research, consulting, training, as well as information and scholarly exchange programs in the fields of social sciences and humanities.

Position on China

WCCS is dedicated to participating and assisting in China's reform process as well as international affairs. The membership of the organization consists primarily of overseas Chinese who are interested in helping the development of their native country.

Comment

Some forums run by WCCS tend to feature perspectives favoring positive U.S. relationships with mainland China, continued MFN treatment, and a moderate U.S. stance on the Taiwan issue that would not seriously upset U.S.-mainland China relations.

Wisconsin Project on Nuclear Arms Control

Founded: 1986
Focus on China: As it relates to nuclear arms control.
Membership/Area of Influence: The project operates in Washington, D.C., under the auspices of the University of Wisconsin.
Activities: Educational, political.
Annual Budget: NA.
Phone: (202) 223-8200 *Fax:* (202) 223-8298

Primary Goals

The project's main goal has been to reduce the risk that exports will be used to make nuclear weapons and the means to deliver them. It carries out research and public education designed to inhibit the spread of nuclear weapons, chemical/biological weapons, and long-range missiles.

Position on China

The Wisconsin Project does not have an official position on China or U.S. policy toward China. As part of its efforts to track proliferation of weapons of mass destruction, the project tracks China's nuclear and missile development programs and its proliferation-related exports.

Comment

By so doing, the Wisconsin Project provides strong evidence to those Americans critical of China and urging conditions on MFN treatment as a means to curb Chinese proliferation activities.

Activities

The Wisconsin Project has worked to influence countries to enforce the export controls contained in international agreements and to comply with the export restrictions of the Nuclear Non-Proliferation Treaty. The project has publicized clandestine nuclear transactions and the weaknesses in agreements or national laws that allow them to happen. Through its research reports, testimony, articles, and work with the press, the project has influenced the export policies of major supplier countries.

In January 1995, the project began to publish the *Risk Report,* a monthly bulletin that tracks the spread of weapons of mass destruction. The *Risk Report* provides U.S. and foreign experts the first unclassified list of "suspect" buyers worldwide—the buyers linked to the spread of nuclear weapons, chemical weapons, and long-range missile technology.

The project has been investigating sales of nuclear—and missile—related technology since 1986 and has identified nearly 1,000 companies and projects linked to proliferation. By listing suspect buyers in sensitive emerging markets, the *Risk Report* helps exporters keep their products out of the wrong hands. It also helps exporters save marketing dollars for sales that governments would not approve. In addition to listing buyers, each issue of the *Risk Report* profiles a country's mass destruction weapons program and includes a list of items the country is trying to buy. The *Risk Report* also covers changes in export control worldwide and other news on proliferation.

Woodrow Wilson International Center for Scholars

Founded: 1968, by Congress.

Focus on China: The Wilson Center has focused on a wide range of topics, including China.

Membership/Area of Influence: The Wilson Center awards forty residential fellowships each year, with the recipients representing a variety of nations, governments, academic and business interests.

Activities: Research/educational.

Funding: The primary source of funding for the Wilson Center comes from an annual congressional appropriation. Other sources of funding come from various organizations, such as the Japan Foundation, the Korea Foundation, the Rockefeller Brothers Fund, and the Henry Luce Foundation.

Phone: (202) 357-1937 *Fax:* (202) 357-4439

Comment

The Wilson Center avoids taking positions on sensitive policy issues. Its recent forums and publications endeavor to cover a wide range of issues and perspectives on China policy questions, including those that would condition or cut off MFN for China as well as those advocating permanent MFN for China. The Wilson Center has done little work recently on Taiwan.

World United Formosans for Independence (WUFI)

Founded: 1970

Focus on China: Entire existence.

Membership/Area of Influence: Chapters in Japan, Europe, Canada, and the United States.

Activities: Political, educational.

Funding: WUFI is supported by private donations.

Phone: (713) 870-1421 *Fax:* (713) 870-9408

Primary Goals

"WUFI is dedicated to the establishment of a free, democratic, and independent Republic of Taiwan in accordance with the principle of self-determination of peoples. We are committed to the fundamental freedoms and human rights and therefore repudiate all forms of foreign dominance and interventions that run counter to the interests of the 20 million Taiwanese people."

Position on China

Taiwan is not a part of China and should not be considered part of the mainland by the PRC. Taiwan should refrain from having relations with China until the PRC recognizes Taiwan as an independent nation.

Activities

Most of WUFI's resources have been dedicated to pushing for change in Taiwan, opposition representation, and free media access. For much of the 1990s, WUFI was busy seeking to have imprisoned opposition leaders freed from Taiwanese jails, to convince the KMT to give up their blacklisting tactics, and to move WUFI's main headquarters to Taiwan. Since the group's inception, WUFI had been banned in Taiwan. Additionally, the group sought to have exiled members of the group gain permission to return home to Taiwan.

Comment

This strongly pro-independence group does not enjoy a big following in Washington.

Chronology

1978
December 15: President Carter announced the United States would establish diplomatic relations with China as of January 1, 1979, and break its official ties with Taiwan.

1985
July 23: During President Li Xiannian's U.S. visit, China and the United States signed an agreement on nuclear power cooperation.
September 23: The Reagan administration withdrew funding for a UN family planning organization because of the group's involvement in family planning efforts in China that reportedly involved coercive abortions.

1988
March 24: It was reported that China had sold CSS-2 intermediate range ballistic missiles to Saudi Arabia.
September 12: President Reagan notified Congress of his intent to approve licenses to export three U.S.-manufactured satellites to China for launch in 1989-1991 on China's Long March rocket.

1989
April 15: Hu Yaobang, former Communist Party chief, died of a heart attack at age seventy-three.
April 22: From 70,000 to 100,000 students staged an unauthorized "sit-in" in Tiananmen Square as Chinese leaders held an official memorial service for Hu Yaobang in the Great Hall of the People.
April 28: Defying official warnings, more than 150,000 demonstrators marched for sixteen hours through Beijing to Tiananmen Square.
May 4: The Chinese government held an official celebration of the seventieth anniversary of the May 4th Movement in the Great Hall of the People in

Tiananmen Square. A crowd estimated at more than 100,000, including students and workers, forced its way through police cordons in Beijing in an unauthorized march to Tiananmen Square to demand more democracy.

May 5: For the first time since demonstrations began, official newspapers in China published details and pictures of demonstrations in Beijing and other cities.

May 18: Crowds estimated at one million people again demonstrated in the streets of Beijing.

May 19: Li Peng made a late-night televised speech, saying he was speaking "for the Party." Li called for measures to "check the turmoil with a firm hand and quickly restore order," ordered army troops into Beijing, and directed protesters to disperse. Diplomatic sources reported that this move had Deng Xiaoping's full support.

May 22: Voice of America officials reported that Chinese authorities began jamming their broadcasts to China for the first time since 1978.

June 4: About 1:30 a.m., Chinese troops using tanks and armored personnel carriers began to fire on the demonstrators in Tiananmen Square. Estimates of civilians killed and wounded ranged as high as 1,000 or more. At Tiananmen Square and other points, numerous soldiers also were wounded, and some killed, by angry mobs.

June 5: At 10:00 a.m., President Bush announced that the United States would take certain steps, including suspension of U.S. military sales to China, in response to the killing of Chinese citizens.

June 9: Paramount leader Deng Xiaoping appeared in public for the first time in more than three weeks to congratulate troops who violently suppressed demonstrations in Tiananmen Square.

June 11: Chinese leaders issued arrest warrants for two dissidents, Fang Lizhi and his wife, Li Shuxian, both of whom had taken refuge in the U.S. Embassy in Beijing.

June 13: China issued an arrest list for student leaders, including Wang Dan and Wuer Kaixi, for inciting a "counterrevolutionary rebellion"—an offense that could carry the death penalty.

June 14: China ordered the expulsion of two U.S. reporters: Al Pessin of the Voice of America and John Pomfret of the Associated Press.

November 21: The president vetoed H.R. 1487, the State Department authorization bill, for reasons unrelated to the package of China sanctions it contained.

November 30: President Bush announced he would pocket veto H.R. 2712, legislation enacted by Congress that would have granted emergency immigration relief to Chinese students in the United States. He stated that the bill was unnecessary because he had that day announced he would take administrative action to effect key portions of the bill.

December 9: It was announced that National Security Advisor Brent Scowcroft and Deputy Secretary of State Lawrence Eagleburger had arrived in Beijing for talks with Chinese leaders. The visit was a surprise, particularly given the administration's ban on high-level exchanges with the PRC.

December 18: It was disclosed that National Security Advisor Scowcroft and Deputy Secretary of State Eagleburger had taken an earlier, secret trip to Beijing in July. According to an article in the *Washington Post*, the trip took place over the July 4th weekend.

December 20: The *Washington Post* reported President Bush's decision to authorize export licenses for three U.S. satellites to be launched on Chinese launch vehicles on the grounds that it was in the "national interest." The satellite licenses had earlier been prohibited both by actions of the president and by legislation recently enacted by Congress. The *Washington Post* reported President Bush's decision to waive sanctions that would have prohibited Export Import Bank lending for China. The lending sanction had been part of legislation enacted into law on November 21, 1989.

1990

January 3: The president certified that the International Development Association (IDA—an entity of the World Bank) had not provided any new loans to China between June 27, 1989, and January 1, 1990. The certification, which Congress had called for the previous year in the Foreign Operations, Export Financing, and Related Programs Appropriations Act of 1990, was a requirement for the release of U.S. funds to IDA.

January 10: China announced the lifting of martial law in Beijing.

January 18: Chinese authorities announced the release of 573 "law-breakers" who took part in the events of Tiananmen Square in June 1989.

January 20: China imposed new restrictions on foreign journalists, including rules that foreign correspondents must "observe journalistic ethics and must not distort facts, fabricate rumors, or use improper means in their reporting."

January 24: By a vote of 390-25, the House overrode the president's veto of H.R. 2712, the Emergency Chinese Immigration Relief Act.

January 25: By a vote of 62-37, the Senate sustained the president's veto of H.R. 2712, the Emergency Chinese Immigration Relief Act.

January 30: By a vote of 98-0, the Senate passed H.R. 3792, the State Department authorization bill containing China sanctions, an earlier version of which had been vetoed by the president for unrelated reasons.

March 2: China agreed in principle to resume U.S. Fulbright scholar exchanges, which it had suspended following the Tiananmen Square crackdown.

May 7: China officially lifted martial law in Lhasa, Tibet, where it had been in place since demonstrations on March 9, 1989.

May 10: China announced the freeing of 211 dissidents jailed after the Tiananmen Square demonstrations.

May 16: Citing cost overruns, China announced it would not proceed with the production phase of its $500 million project with the United States to modernize its F-8 fighter. The arms deal was the largest China had ever concluded with the United States.

May 24: President Bush recommended that China's most-favored-nation (MFN) trading status be extended for one more year.

June 6: It was reported that the United States had complained to China about a report that China was supplying raw materials for chemical weapons to Libya. China announced the release of ninety-seven prisoners detained after the Tiananmen Square demonstrations, bringing the total to 881 announced releases.

June 25: Dissident Fang Lizhi and his wife, Li Shuxian, were permitted to leave China after having been in the U.S. Embassy in Beijing since June 25, 1989. The couple flew to Britain.

July 20: U.S. officials announced that China had agreed to stop arms shipments to the Khmer Rouge guerrillas and supported a disarming of all military forces in Cambodia.

September 22: The eleventh annual Asian Games opened in Beijing.

November 29: China abstained in the United Nations Security Council vote to approve the use of force in the Persian Gulf crisis. A negative vote would have defeated the measure.

November 30: President Bush and Secretary of State Baker met in Washington with China's foreign minister, Qian Qichen, to discuss Sino-American relations. Qian was the highest-ranking official received in Washington since the Tiananmen Square crackdown.

December 17: Assistant Secretary of State Richard Schifter, beginning the first visit to Beijing by a U.S. assistant secretary for human rights, gave Chinese authorities a list of 150 political prisoners and asked for their release.

1991

January 5: The Chinese government announced that seven democracy activists, including four from the government's most-wanted list, had been sentenced to prison terms of two to four years, and two others had been convicted but exempted from punishment.

April 11: An article in the *Washington Post* reported that China was assisting Algeria in a nuclear weapons development program.

April 15: According to the U.S. Commerce Department, the U.S. trade deficit with China in 1990 was $10.4 billion—up from about $6 billion in 1989. The increase meant that China's trade surplus with the United States in 1990 was surpassed only by Japan's and Taiwan's.

April 16: President Bush met with the Dalai Lama, spiritual leader of the Tibetan people, in Washington.

April 26: U.S. Trade Representative Carla Hills cited China and India as "priority foreign countries" for inadequate protection of intellectual-property rights and other violations of U.S. copyright and patent laws under the Special 301 provision of the Omnibus Trade and Competitiveness Act of 1988.

April 30: President Bush announced he would bar the sale of American components for a Chinese domestic-communications satellite because of concerns about Chinese exports of weapons of mass destruction to Middle East countries.

May 9: According to the *New York Times*, Chinese officials agreed to stop exporting prison-made products to the United States.

May 18: The *Washington Post* reported that China's State Education Commission had issued a secret order (Document no. 598) restricting joint research projects with American scholars who assess Chinese public opinion and social problems. The news report also stated that some Chinese scholars were ignoring the restrictions. China sent its second "import mission" to the United States for the purpose of signing contracts to purchase U.S. products, including grain, cotton, chemical fertilizer, and electronic equipment. When the mission left on June 6, it claimed to have signed about $1.2 billion in contracts.

May 24: The Senate adopted S.Con.Res. 41, a resolution expressing the sense of Congress that Tibet is an occupied country whose true representatives are the Dalai Lama and the Tibetan government-in-exile.

May 26: The USTR initiated a "Special 301" investigation of China for violations of U.S. intellectual property rights.

May 27: President Bush, in a Yale University commencement speech, announced formally that he would renew China's MFN status with the United States without any conditions.

May 29: The president submitted his formal notification requesting extension of MFN to China. (Presidential Determination No. 91-36.)

June 19: The *Washington Post* reported that China was "seriously considering" signing the Nuclear Non-Proliferation Treaty (NPT). The United States announced at a U.S. Embassy news conference in Beijing that it would take "unspecified retaliatory measures" if China went ahead with short-range ballistic missile sales to Syria and Pakistan.

July 10: The House, by a vote of 313-112, passed H.R. 2212, amended, placing conditions on extension of MFN to China in 1992.

August 10: China announced it had decided "in principle" to sign the Nuclear Non-Proliferation Pact.

August 15: China's *People's Daily* carried an article attacking former U.S. Ambassador to China James R. Lilley for making statements critical of Beijing's strategy for reunification with Taiwan.

September 4: U.S. Representatives Nancy Pelosi, John Miller, and Ben Jones, on a visit to China, displayed a banner in Tiananmen Square proclaiming "To Those Who Died for Democracy in China." The incident was filmed by ABC, CBS, and CNN cameras. Chinese security guards prevented the members from taking further action, and briefly detained the camera crews.

September 9: Two House subcommittees (Human Rights and International Organizations, and International Economic and Trade Policy) held a joint hearing on Chinese exports made with forced labor.

September 10: The *Washington Post* reported that U.S. Customs officials had seized $3 billion in Chinese textile products and monies that had been shipped to the United States in excess of China's textile quotas.

September 29: In a press conference, a Chinese Foreign Ministry spokesman briefly noted that China welcomed President Bush's September 27 order for unilateral reductions in tactical nuclear weapons.

October 1: Section 134 of the 1990 Immigration Act went into effect, significantly increasing the number of Tibetans permitted to resettle in the United States. The provisions in this section made available 1,000 immigrant visas to "qualified displaced Tibetans." In the past thirty years, only 500 Tibetans had been resettled in the United States.

October 10: The Bush administration ordered an unfair-trade-practices investigation against China under Section 301 of the U.S. trade law, giving China a year to end import barriers before the imposition of possible U.S. sanctions.

November 15: Secretary of State Baker began a three-day visit to Beijing as part of a larger trip through Asia.

December 19: The Bush administration confirmed the lifting of sanctions on the sale of U.S. satellite parts and high-speed computers to China.

December 29: China's National People's Congress voted to sign the Nuclear Nonproliferation Treaty.

1992

January 16: China agreed to improve its protection of patented and copyrighted materials, join the Bern and Geneva conventions, and treat computer software as literary works for copyright purposes.

January 31: President Bush met with Premier Li Peng in New York after a meeting at the United Nations. It was the highest-level U.S.-China meeting since 1989.

March 2: The president vetoed H.R. 2212, a bill to condition China's MFN status.

March 11: The House overrode the president's veto of H.R. 2212 (357-61).
March 18: Two-thirds of the Senate not having concurred, the Senate failed to override the president's veto of H.R. 2212.
June 18: China and the United States reached tentative agreement in a memorandum of understanding (MOU) to prevent the export to America of goods made in Chinese prisons.
July 21: The House passed H.R. 5318, conditioning China's future MFN status (339-62).
August 11: The House passed S. 1731, the U.S.-Hong Kong Relations Act.
September 14: The Democratic presidential candidate, Bill Clinton, commended the U.S. Senate for placing conditions on China's most-favored-nation (MFN) status, and criticized the Bush administration's China policy, saying "The administration policies have led the Chinese leaders to believe they are free to take whatever actions they please without a meaningful response from the United States." The Senate passed H.R. 5318, the U.S.-China Relations Act, conditioning China's MFN status beginning in June 1993.
September 28: The president vetoed H.R. 5318.
September 30: The House overrode the veto of H.R. 5318 (345-74).
October 1: The Senate failed to override the veto of H.R. 5318 (59-40).
November 5: Beijing's first official reaction to the election of Bill Clinton was to congratulate him and to state that any attempt to establish conditions on China's MFN status was "unacceptable to China."
December 2: President-elect Clinton stated that he hoped the United States could play a constructive role in relieving tensions and concerns in Hong Kong.

1993
January 14: China joined 125 other countries in signing the convention banning chemical weapons. Foreign Minister Qian Qichen signed the document in Paris.
January 19: President Clinton named former Ambassador to China Winston Lord as his designee for assistant secretary of state for East Asia and Pacific affairs.
April 13: The British and Chinese governments jointly announced that talks on disputes over Hong Kong would begin on April 22, 1993.
April 29: China and Taiwan signed an accord in Singapore that pledged closer cooperation on trade, technology exchanges, copyright protection, anti-crime efforts, and repatriation of illegal immigrants. The semiofficial talks that led to the agreement were the highest-level exchanges between the two since 1949.
May 11: U.S. Assistant Secretary of State Winston Lord warned Chinese

leaders in Beijing that conditions were likely to be attached to their future MFN status. Lord was the most senior Clinton administration official to have visited China to date.

May 18: Secretary of State Warren Christopher said that the Clinton administration would consider linking China's MFN status to Chinese willingness to end coercive family planning practices, including forced abortions.

May 28: President Clinton, in Presidential Determination 93-23, requested authority to renew China's MFN status for another year. At the same time, however, in Executive Order 12850, the president indicated that he would consider new human rights criteria in considering the MFN renewal in 1994.

August 8: Beijing lodged a strong protest accusing Washington of harassing a Chinese ship, the *Yinhe*. Washington said the ship was believed to be carrying chemical weapons bound for Iran.

August 24: The United States announced it would impose sanctions on China, required by U.S. law, because of China's sale of missile technology to Pakistan. The Chinese government lodged a strong protest.

September 4: An inspection, watched by U.S. observers, of the *Yinhe* revealed no chemical-weapons ingredients on board. The Chinese filed another strong protest after the search.

September 23: The International Olympics Committee rejected Beijing's bid for the 2000 Olympics in favor of the bid of Sydney, Australia.

September 25: National Security Advisor Anthony Lake met China's ambassador to the U.S., Li Diaoyu, to initiate efforts to restore high-level U.S.-China contacts across the board.

October 5: China conducted an underground nuclear test, despite a U.S. call in July for an informal ban on such testing.

October 12: John Shattuck, assistant secretary of state for human rights, visited Beijing to initiate a dialogue on human rights issues.

October 15: Secretary of Agriculture Mike Espy went to Beijing to discuss China's purchases of U.S. grains, especially wheat.

November 1: Assistant Secretary of Defense Charles Freeman began two days of talks in Beijing; they were the highest-level military talks between the two countries since the Tiananmen incident in 1989.

November 3: U.S.-China military talks in Beijing concluded with an agreement to a "modest" agenda of future dialogue and professional exchanges on such topics as international peacekeeping operations and conversion of defense industries to civilian use.

November 17: Two hundred and seventy members of the House of Representatives signed a letter to President Clinton expressing their concern over China's lack of progress in meeting human rights objectives.

November 18: Secretary of State Christopher announced the United States was dropping its opposition to the sale of an $8 million Cray supercomputer to China.

1994

January 6: The United States announced it would slash China's textile quotas by 25 to 30 percent in retaliation for China's illegal textile shipments.

January 20: Chinese officials told U.S. Treasury Secretary Lloyd Bentsen, in Beijing, that they would permit U.S. Customs officials to inspect five prisons alleged to be producing goods for export in violation of U.S. law. The concession put China in compliance with a U.S.-China Memorandum of Understanding (MOU) on prison labor, signed in 1992, which had become moribund after two U.S. site visits.

January 24: Secretary of State Warren Christopher met with China's Foreign Minister Qian Qichen in Paris. Prior to the meeting, the secretary told reporters that China was still not in compliance with President Clinton's conditions for securing MFN in 1994.

January 30: Sen. Sam Nunn, chairman of the Senate Armed Services Committee, said on NBC's "Meet the Press" that withdrawing MFN from China is "too heavy a weapon" when the United States needs China's help in stopping the North Korean nuclear threat.

March 11: Secretary of State Warren Christopher arrived in Beijing for three days of talks about human rights and China's MFN status.

May 26: President Clinton announced that he would be recommending the renewal of China's MFN status despite the fact that China did not make the significant progress on human rights that he had made a condition of MFN renewal in 1993 (Executive Order 12850). In making the announcement, the president said he was "delinking" MFN from China's human rights record. The president also announced that he was imposing an embargo on the import of certain guns and munitions from China.

May 28: An arms import embargo against China went into effect.

June 2: In Presidential Determination 94-26, President Clinton requested an extension of China's most-favored-nation status for another year.

June 10: China conducted a nuclear weapons test. The United States expressed regret.

August 9: The House passed legislation extending MFN to China and delinking it from human rights concerns, and rejected a bill by Representative Pelosi to limit the extension of MFN to China.

August 17: Secretary of Defense Perry met with a visiting deputy chief of staff of the Chinese Army in Washington.

September 4: Secretary of Commerce Brown left China after a visit marked by the signing of over $5 billion worth of contracts involving U.S. business.

September 7: The Clinton administration disclosed a Taiwan policy review that promised modestly increased contacts with Taiwan. Beijing issued an official protest.

October 4: The United States and China issued a joint statement on China's adherence to the Missile Technology Control Regime. The United States promised to waive sanctions imposed on August 23, 1993, allowing the export of high-technology satellites to China.

October 7: China conducted a nuclear weapons test, its second in 1994.

October 19: Defense Secretary Perry ended four days of talks in Beijing, resuming high-level military ties that had been suspended in 1989 as a result of the Tiananmen Square crackdown.

November 1: The administration lifted sanctions it had imposed on China on August 24, 1993, after China's export to Pakistan of items listed in category II of the Annex of the Missile Technology Control Regime (MTCR).

December 7: The *Los Angeles Times* reported that China had threatened to end commercial agreements with the United States if the Clinton administration did not acquiesce in China's entry into GATT by year's end.

1995

January 15: Assistant Secretary Shattuck left Beijing after fruitless talks on human rights.

February 1: The U.S. trade deficit with China grew in 1994 to almost $30 billion.

February 4: The United States imposed trade sanctions worth over $1 billion because of an intellectual property rights dispute with China; China immediately announced comparable sanctions against the United States.

February 22: China protested U.S. support for a UN resolution critical of Chinese human rights conditions.

February 26: A U.S.-Chinese agreement on intellectual property rights disputes was signed, averting a U.S.-China trade conflict threatening $2 billion in annual trade.

March 12: The United States and China signed an eight-point agreement to assist China's entry into the World Trade Organization.

March 22: A U.S. warship visited China for the first time in six years.

March 27: Clinton administration efforts to come up with a code of conduct for U.S. firms doing business in China and elsewhere were criticized by congressional and other U.S. human rights advocates.

March 31: A legally required U.S. State Department report of March 31, 1995, warned of potential uncertainties in Hong Kong's legal and political systems if greater Sino-British progress on these issues were not made prior to July 1, 1997.

April 6: A Chinese Foreign Ministry spokesman criticized the "irresponsible comments" of the U.S. State Department's report on Hong Kong.

May 2: By a vote of 396-0, the House passed H.Con.Res. 53, a bill expressing the sense of Congress that Taiwan's president, Lee Teng-hui, be allowed to visit the United States.

May 5: By a vote of 97-1, the Senate passed H.Con.Res. 53, a bill expressing the sense of Congress that Taiwan's president, Lee Teng-hui, be allowed to visit the United States.

May 9: State Department officials said that a visit to the United States by Taiwan's president, Lee Teng-hui, would have "serious consequences for U.S. foreign policy."

May 22: President Clinton agreed to allow Taiwan's president to make a private visit to his alma mater in the United States. Beijing protested strongly.

May 26: China postponed the planned visit of its defense minister to the United States.

June 2: In Presidential Determination 95-23, President Clinton requested an extension of China's most-favored-nation status for one year.

June 16: China withdrew its ambassador from the United States in protest over the U.S. decision to allow Taiwan President Lee Teng-hui to visit the United States.

June 19: Chinese authorities detained Harry Wu, although he had a valid U.S. passport and Chinese visa, at the Chinese border post of Horgas.

July 20: The House passed H.R. 2058, the China Policy Act of 1995, by a vote of 460-10, and tabled H.J.Res. 96 (denying extension of MFN) by a vote of 321-107.

August 15: China began ten days of naval exercises and live ballistic missile test firings in the Taiwan Strait.

August 24: China convicted Harry Wu of spying, sentenced him to 15 years in prison, and expelled him from the country.

September 4: The 4th U.N. International Women's Conference began in Beijing and Huairou, a suburb of Beijing. Hillary Clinton attended the conference.

October 24: President Clinton and China's president and party secretary, Jiang Zemin, held a "summit meeting" in New York to try to resolve U.S.-China tensions.

November 17: Assistant Secretary of Defense Joseph Nye visited Beijing.

November 29: China confirmed a six-year-old boy, Gyaincain Norbu, as Tibet's eleventh Panchen Lama, rejecting the Dalai Lama's choice of another six-year-old.

1996

January 19: China expelled a U.S. military attaché.

January 24: The *New York Times* reported on a series of explicit warnings from Chinese leaders to the United States over the likelihood of military action in the Taiwan Strait.

February 6: Wang Jun, president of China's CITIC and chairman of Poly Technologies (a Chinese military company), attended a White House reception with President Clinton. President Clinton issued a waiver of restrictions on U.S. satellite exports to China, contained in the Foreign Relations Authorization Act (P.L. 101-246), saying that it was in the national interest to export U.S.-origin satellites to China.

February 22: CIA Director John Deutch complained in an open hearing about Chinese sales of cruise missiles to Iran, ring magnets to Pakistan, and M-11 missiles to Pakistan.

March 8: PRC military forces began conducting ballistic missile exercises targeting two impact areas near Taiwan. The actions were vigorously condemned by the Clinton administration and Congress.

March 10: Amid repeated U.S. official condemnations of PRC missile tests and planned live-fire exercises in the Taiwan Strait, the Pentagon disclosed that two U.S. carrier battle groups had been ordered to the area.

March 22: Secretary of Defense William Perry postponed the visit of China's defense minister to the United States.

March 23: In Taiwan's first popular election for president, Lee Teng-hui was elected by 54 percent of the vote in a four-candidate field.

April 30: The USTR designated China as a "priority foreign country" under "Special 301" trade sanctions provisions for not fully complying with a February 1995 intellectual property rights agreement.

May 10: The U.S. State Department declared that no sanctions would be imposed on China linked to Chinese sales of "ring magnets" to Pakistan, and the Export-Import (Exim) Bank resumed normal consideration of loans for U.S. exports to China.

May 11: China pledged not to provide assistance to unsafeguarded nuclear facilities.

May 15: The USTR declared it would impose sweeping sanctions on China by June 17 unless China took adequate steps to enforce the terms of its 1995 agreement with the United States on intellectual property rights.

May 20: President Clinton announced that he would be requesting an extension of China's most-favored-nation (MFN) trading status.

May 22: Federal law enforcement agents began seeking arrests of Chinese arms dealers for smuggling 2,000 AK-47 assault weapons through Oakland on March 18, 1996. According to court papers, two Chinese state-owned arms-trading companies were involved: Poly Technologies and Norinco.

May 31: In Presidential Determination 96-29, President Clinton extended China's most-favored-nation trading status for one year.

June 11: In an interview with the *Financial Times*, China's Premier Li Peng warned that China would give more contracts to non-American companies unless the United States stopped pressuring China to change its policies.

June 12: Assistant Secretary of State Winston Lord, testifying before the House Ways and Means Committee, sharply criticized Japan and U.S. European allies for exploiting U.S.-China tensions for their own economic benefit.

June 17: U.S. Trade Representative Charlene Barshevsky announced that the United States was now satisfied that China was taking steps to honor its 1995 commitments on intellectual property rights and that, as a result, the United States would not carry out its threat to impose sanctions on China.

June 21: In Presidential Determination 96-33, President Clinton extended the U.S.-China trade agreement through January 31, 1998.

June 27: On June 27, 1996, the House rejected (141-286) H.J.Res. 182, a resolution that would have disapproved the president's recommendation to extend China's MFN status for another year. At the same time, the House agreed to a compromise resolution requiring four House committees to hold hearings before September 1, 1996, about various ongoing problems in U.S.-China relations.

July 10: U.S. National Security Advisor Anthony Lake wrapped up a visit to China.

July 24: The United States and China announced a series of high-level visits in an effort to improve U.S.-China relations. These included visits to China by Secretary of State Warren Christopher, Undersecretary of State Lynn Davis, and Director of the Arms Control and Disarmament Agency John Holum; and visits to the United States by Defense Minister Chi Haotian and Security Adviser Liu Huaqiu.

July 30: The PRC announced a moratorium on nuclear testing after its latest test on July 29.

September 2: News reports indicated that China had begun a serious crackdown on Muslim separatists in Xinjiang Province.

October 30: China sentenced dissident Wang Dan to eleven years in prison.

November 5: Undersecretary of State for Arms Control and International Security Affairs Lynn Davis concluded a visit to Beijing.

November 19: U.S. Secretary of State Warren Christopher went to China.

November 24: President Clinton held an official meeting with President Jiang Zemin at the APEC leaders' meeting in Manila, where they agreed to exchange state visits within the next two years.

December 5: Assistant Secretary of State Winston Lord voiced opposition to China's efforts to disband Hong Kong's elected legislature and replace it with a provisional body. China's Minister of Defense, General Chi Haotian, began a thirteen-day visit to the United States. During his visit, the general generated controversy by defending the government's military action during the 1989 Tiananmen incident, denying that any deaths occurred in Tiananmen Square and refusing to renounce the use of force to reclaim Taiwan.

December 9: President Clinton and Secretary of Defense William Perry met with visiting Chinese Minister of Defense General Chi Haotian. Beijing agreed in principle to allow U.S. warship visits to Hong Kong after its return to China.

December 11: China's Selection Committee chose Hong Kong shipping magnate Tung Chee-hwa as Hong Kong's first post-colonial chief executive.

December 20: President Clinton said that it was inappropriate for him to have met in February 1996 at the White House with Mr. Wang Jun, the head of a Chinese investment company and Chinese weapons trading company, which was under investigation for illicit arms trading and whose representatives have been charged with smuggling military assault rifles into the United States.

December 21: China's Selection Committee chose a sixty-member provisional legislature to replace Hong Kong's elected Legislative Council on July 1, 1997.

1997

January 14: President Jiang Zemin met in Beijing with a twenty-two-member U.S. congressional delegation.

January 15: During a repatriation ceremony in Beijing, China returned to U.S. officials the remains of airmen killed in the country during World War II.

January 28: In a press conference, President Clinton said that his policy of "constructive engagement" with China had not brought about the progress on human rights that he had hoped for.

January 30: The State Department issued its 1997 human rights report, which accused China of silencing virtually all public dissent in 1996 through intimidation, exile, imposition of prison terms, administrative detention, or house arrest.

February 2: The United States and China reached a four-year textile agreement extending current quotas for Chinese textile and apparel exports to the United States but providing reduced quotas in categories where repeated textile transshipments had occurred. China also promised to allow U.S. textile and apparel products greater access to the Chinese market.

February 6: China's official media charged that the U.S. State Department Report on Human Rights contained "malicious attacks on and lies about China's human rights situation."

February 13: The *Washington Post* reported that the Justice Department's investigation into improper political fund-raising practices had revealed through sensitive intelligence information illegal attempts by the Chinese government to funnel contributions from foreign sources to the Democratic National Committee before the 1996 presidential campaign. Beijing dismissed the allegations as a "fabrication." President Clinton said the allegations must be "thoroughly investigated."

February 16: Congressional leaders reported that committees investigating improper political fund-raising practices would expand their inquiries to include allegations of the Chinese government's efforts to buy administration influence.

February 19: Beijing announced that Deng Xiaoping, 92, had died that day.

February 24: Secretary of State Madeleine Albright held talks in Beijing.

February 28: The *Washington Post* reported that the FBI was conducting a broader investigation, beyond possible election-law violations, into whether representatives of China attempted to buy influence among members of Congress through illegal campaign contributions and payments from Chinese-controlled businesses.

March 14: U.S. Trade Representative Charlene Barshefshy stated at a congressional hearing that China must make more significant market access concessions before it can join the World Trade Organization.

March 24: Vice President Gore began a visit to China—the highest-level U.S.-visit to China since 1989.

March 27: The Dalai Lama, the spiritual leader of Tibet, visited with Taiwan's President Lee Teng-hui in Taipei. The visit was denounced by Beijing.

March 28: Speaker of the House Newt Gingrich met with senior Chinese leaders in Beijing.

April 1: Federal law enforcement officials confirmed that "substantial" wire transfers were made in 1995 and 1996 from the Bank of China to Charles Trie, an Arkansas businessman under investigation for questionable contributions to President Clinton's and other officials' election campaigns. At issue were allegations of illegal U.S. election campaign contributions by foreign governments attempting to influence U.S. policy. The Chinese government, which owns the Bank of China, denied any wrongdoing.

April 21: The Dalai Lama, the spiritual leader of Tibet, began a four-day visit to Washington, D.C.

May 19: President Clinton announced that he would be requesting an extension of China's MFN trading status.

June 24: The House disapproved (259-173) a joint resolution ending MFN treatment for China.

July 1: Chinese President Jiang Zemin and Premier Li Peng participated in ceremonies in Hong Kong marking its transition to Chinese rule.

July 8: Chairman Fred Thompson began Senate Government Affairs Committee hearings on campaign financing irregularities with charges against the Chinese government's alleged illegal efforts to influence U.S. election politics.

September 18: The Chinese Communist Party's 15th Congress ended in Beijing.

October 30: Chinese President Jiang Zemin left Washington after two days of talks with President Clinton along with other U.S. government leaders.

Selected Readings

Barnett, A. Doak, et. al., *Developing a Peaceful, Stable, and Cooperative Relationship with China*. New York. National Committee on American Foreign Policy, 1996.

Barnett, A. Doak, *U.S.-China Relations: Time for a New Beginning—Again*. Washington. Johns Hopkins School of Advanced International Studies, 1994.

Bernstein, Richard and Ross Munro. *The Coming Conflict with China*. New York. Knopf, 1997.

Christensen, Thomas. "Chinese Realpolitik," *Foreign Affairs*. September-October 1996, pp. 37-52.

Cox, Mary-Lea. "Trade and Investment in East Asia: Political and Economic Opportunities and Constraints," Woodrow Wilson Center, Asia Program, *Occasional Paper*, no. 73, April 1997.

Dallek, Robert. *The American Style of Foreign Policy: Cultural Politics and Foreign Affairs*. New York. Oxford U. Press, 1990.

De Conde, Alexander. *Ethnicity, Race and American Foreign Policy*. Boston. Northeastern University Press, 1992.

Destler, I. M. *American Trade Politics*. Washington. Institute for International Economics, 1992.

Frank, Thomas M. and Edward Weisband. *Foreign Policy by Congress*. New York. Oxford University Press, 1979.

Fuchs, Lawrence, ed. *American Ethnic Politics*. New York. Harper and Row, 1968.

Harding, Harry. *Public Engagement in American Foreign Policy*. New York. The American Assembly, 1995.

Hughes, Barry B. *The Domestic Context of American Foreign Policy*. San Francisco. W. H. Freeman and Company, 1978.

Lampton, David M. "America's China Policy in the Age of the Finance Minister: Clinton Ends Linkage." *The China Quarterly*. September 1994, pp. 597-621.

Levering, Ralph B. "Public Opinion, Foreign Policy and American Politics Since the 1960s." *Diplomatic History*. Summer 1989.

Madsen, Richard. *China and the American Dream*. Berkeley. University of California Press, 1996.

Mathias, Charles McC., Jr., "Ethnic Groups and Foreign Policy." *Foreign Affairs*. Summer 1981, pp. 975-98.

Nathan, Andrew and Robert Ross. *The Great Wall and Empty Fortress*. New York. Norton, 1997.

Oksenberg, Michel, and Elizabeth Economy. *Shaping U.S.-China Relations: A Long-Term Strategy*. New York. Council on Foreign Relations, 1997.

Osborne, David. "Lobbying for Japan Inc." *New York Times Magazine*. December 4, 1983, pp. 133-39.

Overholt, William. "China after Deng." *Foreign Affairs*. May-June 1996.

Pillsbury, Michael, ed. *Chinese Views of Future Warfare*. Washington. National Defense University Press, 1997.

Piper, Don C. and Ronald J. Terchek, eds. *Interaction: Foreign Policy and Public Policy*. Washington. American Enterprise Institute, 1983.

Putnam, Robert D. "Diplomacy and Domestic Politics: The Logic of Two-Level Game." *International Organization*. Vol. 42. No. 3. Summer 1988, pp. 427-60.

Pye, Lucian. "Money Politics and Transitions to Democracy in East Asia." *Asian Survey*. March 1997, pp. 213-28.

Ricci, David M. *The Transformation of American Politics: The New Washington and the Rise of Think Tanks*. New Haven. Yale U. Press, 1993.

Robinson, Thomas W. "America in Taiwan's Post-Cold War Foreign Relations." *The China Quarterly*. December 1996, pp. 1340-61.

Rosenau, James N., ed. *Domestic Sources of Foreign Policy*. New York. Free Press, 1967.

Said, Abdul Aziz, ed. *Ethnicity and U.S. Foreign Policy*. New York. Praeger, 1977.

Shambaugh, David. "The United States and China: Cooperation or Confrontation," *Current History*. September 1997, pp. 241-45.

Shinn, James, ed. *Weaving the Net: Conditional Engagement with China*. New York. Council on Foreign Relations, 1996.

Smith, James A. *The Idea Brokers: Think Tanks and the Rise of the New Policy Elite*. New York. Free Press, 1991.

Stern, Paula. *Water's Edge: Domestic Politics and the Making of American Foreign Policy*. Westport, Conn. Greenwood Press, 1979.

Stokes, Bruce. "Playing Favorites." *National Journal*. March 26, 1994, pp. 713-16.

Stone, Peter H. "China Connections." *National Journal*. March 26, 1994, pp. 708-12.

Tierney, John. "Interest Group Involvement in Congressional Foreign and Defense Policy," in Randall B. Ripley and James M. Lindsay, eds. *Congress Resurgent: Foreign and Defense Policy on Capitol Hill*. Ann Arbor. U. of Michigan Press, 1993, pp. 89-111.

Trice, Robert H. *Interest Groups and the Foreign Policy Process*. London. Sage Publications, 1976.

Tucker, Nancy Bernkopf. *Taiwan, Hong Kong and the United States, 1945-1992: Uncertain Friendships*. New York. Twayne, 1994.

Vogel, Ezra, ed. *Living with China: U.S.-China Relations in the 21st Century*. New York. Norton, 1997.

Index

Index

About the Author

Robert Sutter has specialized in Asian and Pacific affairs and U.S. foreign policy with the Congressional Research Service of the Library of Congress since 1977. He is currently the Senior Specialist in International Politics with the Congressional Research Service. In his government service of over thirty years, Dr. Sutter has held a variety of analytical and supervisory positions with the Central Intelligence Agency, the Department of State, the Senate Foreign Relations Committee, and the Congressional Research Service. He received a Ph.D. in History and East Asian Languages from Harvard University. He teaches regularly at Georgetown, George Washington, and Johns Hopkins Universities. He has published eleven books and numerous articles dealing with contemporary East Asian countries and their relations with the United States. The viewpoints expressed in this book are the author's, not those of the Congressional Research Service.